Common Sense
for **Horses**

Common Sense
for Horses
& Horse Sense for Humans

Deborah Morgan

TATE PUBLISHING
AND ENTERPRISES, LLC

Published by Tate Publishing & Enterprises, LLC
127 E. Trade Center Terrace | Mustang, Oklahoma 73064 USA
1.888.361.9473 | www.tatepublishing.com

Tate Publishing is committed to excellence in the publishing industry. The company reflects the philosophy established by the founders, based on Psalm 68:11,
"The Lord gave the word and great was the company of those who published it."

Published in the United States of America

ISBN: 978-1-63449-476-2
Sports & Recreation / Equestrian
14.07.03

This book is dedicated to and in memory and honor of my parents, the Rev. Charles E. and Dorothy J. Morgan, who were the greatest influences in my life. They provided me with a Christian upbringing and a legacy of Christ-like love. I never knew it was possible to miss someone so much for so long.

"Thank you for this little farm where I reside and which is now known as Gentle Spirit Stables."

Contents

Preface... ...9
Introduction "What in the World
 is Natural Horsemanship and Horse
 Whispering Anyway?"..................................... 11

Section 1
My Horse Dream

My Horse Life: Childhood Dreams....................... 17
My Horse Life as an Adult..................................... 23
Don't Expect Help and
 Encouragement from Your Family or Friends............... 35

Section 2
Farm Photos

Horse Life in Action - Common Sense Applied 41

Section 3
Your Horse Dream

So Now You're Ready to Buy Your Horse 75
 Which Horse Discipline.................................... 75
 Which Breed 76
 Sources of Information 77
 To Board or to Build....................................... 77
 Other Budget Considerations............................... 85
 Vetting.. 85
 Forage and Fresh Water.................................... 86
 Feed.. 87

Barefoot or Horse Shoes 90
You've Found the Horse of Your Dreams 95
    Get a Consultation / Trainer 95
    Take a Ride or Two 97
    Try Out a Few Horses You Like 98
    Listen to Your Intuition and Your Trainer 98
    Know Your Budget and Stick With It! 99
    Negotiate: It's a Buyer's Market 99
Bringing Your New Baby Home 101
Transportation, Insurance, Coggins 101

Section 4
Working with Your Horse:
The Practical Side

The Gentle Spirit REWARD Technique 105
    What to Do Next? 105
    The Basics 110
Common Sense Tips and Tidbits
Make Your Horse Life Happier and Simpler! 115
    Preventing Colic 115
    Traveling and Trailering 117
    Grooming 120
    Bugs and Pests 124
    Warnings from Your Horse 126
    Miscellaneous 128
Sample Contracts 135
    Liability Waiver 137
    Boarding Contract 138
    Horse Lease Agreement 145
Epilogue 149
Acknowledgments 151

Preface

This writing has been inspired from and through my own personal interactions and ongoing relationship with God, family, and horses. Most people have a natural regard for the innate beauty and somewhat mystical attraction between humans and horses, although some folks such as myself experience a much deeper desire to interact and seek out all things equine.

From early childhood, I can still vividly recall my original "dream horses" including but not limited to: National Velvet, Flicka, Black Beauty, Silver, Trigger, Buttermilk, and even the comical Mr. Ed. To this day, I am interested in every movie, television production, and book which features the equine and its partnership with the human. It is with substantial humility that I acknowledge how this passion for horses has intertwined with and impacted my life and my family relationships since childhood.

Horse ownership requires a commitment akin to the undertaking one makes when adding a new member to the family; without a prior understanding in regard to this sometimes overwhelming responsibility, one's personal life and relationships will suffer. Therefore, my ultimate goal in the rendering of a more common sense approach to horse-keeping is intended to encourage, advise, and provide a somewhat simple method toward fulfilling *your* horse dream, without the sacrifice of the more important relationships in your life to include God, family, and friends.

Introduction
"What in the World is Natural Horsemanship and Horse Whispering Anyway?"

In order to more fully comprehend my references to the relationship which can exist between human and horse, it is necessary to understand the terms *natural horsemanship* and *horse whispering*.

Wikipedia defines this term as follows:

> Natural horsemanship, colloquially known as horse whispering, is a collective term for a variety of horse training techniques which have seen rapid growth in popularity since the 1980's. The techniques vary in their precise tenets but generally share principles of developing a rapport with horses, using communication techniques derived from observation of free-roaming horses, and rejecting abusive training methods.

My personal definition of natural horsemanship (which is synonymous with horse whispering) is a little simpler:

> I define it as the somewhat *unnatural* understanding and communication between human and horse. It is a combination of one's passion to understand how to best allow a horse into our own mind and our willingness to figure out what the horse is thinking—an ability which evolves throughout the relationship between horse and

human. It requires from humans the four *P* words: *passion, patience, perseverance, and practice.*

Natural horsemanship is definitely not created by man, nor is it new. For hundreds of years, our Native American ancestors likely used their own form of horse whispering and natural methods of working with their own horses. In fact, there are thousands of children who, over the years, have used their own methods of natural horsemanship in figuring out how to get their stubborn little ponies to stop and go. And I am certain there have been hundreds, if not thousands, of "closet horse whisperers" in the cowboy industry—those men who "became one" with their horse in the course of their day-to-day interaction. In fact, I suspect there were many cowboys who loved their horses and shared more of themselves with their horse than with any human. They would likely argue that *horses* are man's best friend rather even than their canine buddies.

The most humorous reference to horse whispering for myself actually came from my ex-husband, who stated,

> I used to think that horse whispering had something to do with the communication between man and horse; however, in the course of my wife's path in purchasing her horses to the fulfillment of her heart's desire I have come to realize that "horse whispering" actually refers to the literal whispering that occurs regarding the cash required in order to satisfy her horse habit!

This somewhat funny reference does actually bear some relevance, as you will figure out in the process of your own "horse quest."

You will definitely find yourself displaying some addictive behaviors, including but not limited to: directing cash toward equine products which you heretofore had never considered; redirecting vacation trends toward locations which are horse-related; experiencing a preoccupation with all things equine (even in your dreams); choosing to do stinky horse chores rather than watch your favorite movie (which, by the way, will no longer be your favorite movie if it doesn't include horses); interacting and enthusiastically conversing for hours on end with complete strangers who share your passion; checking out every website that offers horse photos, horse products, horse barns, horse trailers, etc.; and the list continues. At some point, you may recognize some of these traits in yourself, at which time you likely will be whispering on occasion when discussing horse matters around folks who may not be horse enthusiasts, thereby becoming a sort of "equine addict."

If you find yourself interested in or recognize yourself in any of the above-named activities, then this is the book for you! My goal is to help you fulfill that desire within as it pertains to your horse dreams, while at the same time maintaining a healthy balance between this strong addictive behavior and your family and workplace life. Common sense and simplicity in horse keeping is actually possible, and is required if one is to maintain a healthy home life.

I hope that this writing will be relative, inspirational, and worthwhile for you as you begin (or continue in) your amazing horse quest.

Happy People, Happy Horses

A righteous man cares for the needs of his animal.

Proverbs 12:10, niv

Section 1
My Horse Dream

My Horse Life:
Childhood Dreams

My first memory of a horse occurred at the age of five (almost fifty-six years ago) and was actually a hobby horse. I can still vividly recall how much I wanted to ride that horse. My mother told me I was too old for a hobby horse. Little did she know that the real thing would be my goal from that moment forward.

I also recall having mules on the farm which were used for plowing and pulling trailers; they were a source of amazement to me with their huge ears and apparent ability to ignore the many farming distractions around them. What wonderful creatures they were, but to me untouchable, as my hovering mother and aunt would not allow me near them for fear I might get a swift kick or bite.

And then there were the stories Daddy told about the horse he owned as a boy and young man, stories which were so powerful in my mind's eye that I could vividly picture every moment of his eight-mile rides back and forth to the small town of Bailey, where he would buy needed groceries and items from the local hardware store. Unfortunately, my mother heard those same stories, particularly recalling the time his horse stumbled at a full gallop, spilling him onto the hard dirt road—more fuel for the "protective hovering mother gene" which was especially relevant to me as an only child.

In an effort to satisfy what they perceived as my earnest need for a farm animal with which to bond, they bought me a goat—*a goat*!—and that goat actually ended up inside my uncle's water well. Yikes! He evidently thought it to be a good hideaway spot from chasing dogs, failing to recognize it was a deep hole filled with water. He was discovered about a week later when my uncle's well water failed to pump. No more goats for me!

I *was* allowed to have a dog, however, and still do. I loved dogs, and still do as well, but neither did *they* satisfy that equine gene which had evidently been passed on to me from my dad. So of course, I continued to ask, beg, plead, and dream of getting my own horse. I recall lying in bed at night, especially around Christmas, picturing myself awakening on Christmas morning to find a fully saddled Shetland pony waiting for me just outside my back door. I never told my parents, or Santa, about that dream, because I knew it wasn't likely to come true. But I knew I could always keep my dream alive if I didn't tell.

Evidently, my unending quest for a horse did make a small chink in that mother armor, and she finally agreed for me to take riding lessons. *Yea!* I was ten years old and enrolled for a semester of group riding lessons at Meredith College in Raleigh, which was about an hour's drive from our home. The lessons were offered to youngsters as well as to Meredith's college enrollees on Saturday mornings. Meredith had a beautiful campus with a huge horse barn and obviously a large variety of equine which included ponies, English-trained mounts, old horses and young horses. I thought I was in heaven! Myself and two other young girls who I didn't really know well were carpooled to Raleigh every Saturday morning for that one winter semester, rain or shine. This was the beginning of my first hands-on horse experience. It took. Once I had ridden those ponies bareback and plodded around on Big Mama, who was so huge and whose girth was so wide I could barely touch her sides with my legs, I knew I would always be in love with horses.

On cold rainy Saturdays, we were required to sit in the tack room and be lectured regarding the various equipment and tack necessary for horse endeavors; all I can recall from that experience is that I loved the smell of leather in the room. That took as well.

Other days our instructor taught us the basics of English riding; I recall being assigned a rather disagreeable horse named Belle. I was not confident while riding her, but the posting lessons on her stayed with me, and thankfully, I never took a spill. The one distinct memory I have as well is that of the conversation between my mother and the instructor, after which I was only allowed to ride Big Mama. I think I can figure out how that came to be! I didn't care, however, because Big Mama always took good care of her riders, although I did have to deal with the slight stigma attached to Big Mama mountees; everyone knew that she was assigned to the less capable students. I finished that semester knowing only slightly more about riding than I had known at the beginning, but my heart was full of happy, and I knew I was one step closer to having my own horse.

And then it happened. *Daddy found a horse for me!* He had purchased a four-year-old green broke mare named Ginger with saddle and tack which he had apparently bought at a good price. It wasn't that Shetland pony with the beautiful mane and saddle I had always dreamed it would be, but I thought she was the most beautiful horse I had ever seen—because I knew she belonged to me. I didn't hesitate to get right inside that stall with her as she munched on hay, standing quiet as a mouse for me. Now that's the kind of horse whispering which naturally occurs between a child and her horse. Until, enter another hovering aunt, who scolded me for being inside the stall and insisted that I shouldn't be allowed to go in the stall lest I be trampled to death by the wild beast within. Naturally, my aunt informed Mother of the less than calm trailer delivery which had occurred earlier that day and of how my new best friend, Ginger, had displayed a bit of rodeo bronco upon her arrival. No more unsupervised horseplay for me!

Eventually, my dad built a run-in shed for Ginger at our house, and we were able to bring her a little closer. I was never allowed to ride her without an adult on hand, however, likely the result of her having "dumped" my mother on a memorable Sunday afternoon ride. Hmmm…perhaps they did not "whisper" together enough! My experience with Ginger never matured into what I had hoped; Mother's fears had infiltrated my mind somewhat and most of the lessons I learned from Ginger had to do with the responsibility of horse-keeping chores. As I grew into my teenage years and early adulthood, Daddy chose to find a new home for Ginger; after all, he had become her primary caretaker and horses require lots of attention and upkeep as well as cash.

In retrospect, a little more "common sense for horses and horse sense for humans" would have been appropriate:

"Daddy bought the wrong horse for the right child."

Lessons to be Learned

1. Don't buy a young, untrained (green broke) horse for an inexperienced child. Child-safe means *years* under saddle and in most cases "long in the tooth." The oldest, slowest dead-broke horse you can find is where you should begin and end the search for your child's first horse.
2. Don't buy a horse compatible with someone else's riding skill level. A horse is only as good as its rider. The calm, well-behaved horse you see someone else ride can turn into a bucking bronco rodeo horse with an inexperienced rider.
3. Don't purchase a horse for a "good deal." Bad choice. If a horse is "cheap" or a "good deal," there is usually a reason. Make the initial purchase a wise one. A little more money up front can sometimes mean a lot less money spent for training later on.
4. Don't purchase a horse you or the prospective new owner has never ridden. Different horses have a different "feel." It is not possible to know if you are comfortable on a

particular horse unless you actually ride that horse a few times.

5. Don't purchase a horse because it's "pretty." Beauty is in the eye of the beholder, and when the beauty of the horse comes from within, just as with humans, it will mark the beginning of a long and loving relationship. The prettiest horses on the outside can turn into absolute demons if you've not used good common sense and lots of horse sense before you make that purchase!

Don't follow your heart. "The heart is deceitful above all things"

(Jeremiah 17:9, kjv)

My Horse Life as an Adult

Fast forward some thirty-five years from the time I first laid eyes on Ginger—there I was at age forty-five and still longing for my very own horse, again. My horse addiction had begun to resurface shortly after my youngest child had moved away to college, and the old "empty nest syndrome" had set in.

Seeking to legitimately fill that longing for companionship, and now having become a city dweller, I initially sought out the perfect dog, sincerely believing that a dog could fill the "horse void" that still occupied a vast portion of my heart. The Internet provided hours of research options, and I ultimately determined that the perfect canine companion for me would be a miniature American husky. I based this decision, of course, almost exclusively on the look of the dog. Once more, I found myself explaining my need for an animal, except this time I was trying to convince my then-husband—a man who was totally at odds with having any type of animal which would require my time and limit our newly found freedom. Hence, no children in the house; no dogs in the house.

My equine addiction continued to beckon (since I had been forbidden to purchase a dog), and unbeknownst to my husband, I sought out all horses available for sale within a 150-mile radius, and then extended beyond state boundaries to learn every detail about a little-known breed to our locale: the Haflinger. I downloaded Haflinger screen savers and inquired about every potential Haflinger horse for sale on the East Coast. Eventually, I determined that if I were to have any potential success in coaxing him (my husband) to agree in regard to the purchase of a horse, I would be better served by locating a horse in closer proximity.

Which, of course, I was readily able to do. There are plenty of horses on the market at any given time, and it's always a buyers' market when it relates to buying horses.

Although I was not able to locate a Haflinger for sale nearby, I was able to find a palomino American Quarter Horse, which was advertised for sale in the local newspaper. Palomino—a color, not a breed; that was what I had really wanted. Haflingers are palomino in color. Every little "horse girl" at some point in time wants a palomino. I immediately made an appointment to see this horse and quietly set about the business of buying my first horse as an adult.

The palomino for sale was pretty, but once I arrived on site, I realized I was at a horse broker's farm. There was a horse (many horses, in fact) of a different color which struck my eye—Ole Blue-Eyes, a.k.a. Cowboy, who was soon to become my first horse as an adult. I had to pass his stall on the way to the palomino's paddock, and I was starstruck with my first look into those sky blue eyes of his. Until that moment, I hadn't known horses were ever blessed with blue eyes. And of course, the horse broker had seen me coming a mile away. She remarked on his beautiful blue eyes, and as a sidebar mentioned another potential buyer who was interested in him. I fell for her sales pitch "lock, stock, and barrel." Cowboy became, at that very moment, the horse for me.

It didn't seem relevant to me at the time that I had never seen him under saddle prior to the purchase; I committed to buying him on the spot. The broker conveniently offered him up for me to ride over a period of several months while I was preparing the barn and stall for him on my dad's family farm. Cowboy was always saddled and ready for me to ride every time I visited. They provided me with a large round pen area as well as a stable boy to attend to saddle and tack. How accommodating! With only a few minor exceptions, my rides were uneventful, and I was elated as I looked forward to bringing him home.

In retrospect, I should have recognized that the broker's barn hand always planned in advance for my visits, and never once was it suggested that I ride Cowboy outside the riding arena. I heard numerous stories of how calm he was and how he had been ridden during a local event known as Mule Days, together with hundreds of other mules and horses, confirming in my mind that he was a bombproof, settled, mature gelding. I'm surprised they didn't try to convince me he was used for therapy at nursing homes and day care centers! (That description was actually saved for the Shetland pony I later purchased for my granddaughters!)

Everything was wonderful and exciting as I prepared to bring Cowboy to his "forever home." And following his arrival, all was well as long as he was ridden in an enclosed area. His ground manners were excellent, and of course, those blue eyes were still just as beautiful as they had been upon first glance, but it is nothing short of a miracle that I survived those first rides on our farm. Outside the pasture he became a maniac, displaying a studdish horse attitude from, well, certainly not a heavenly place. This was the horse I bought, but definitely *not* the horse I *thought* I had bought. What to do?!

The first thing I did after realizing that there were some issues with Cowboy's behavior was to call the broker. I attempted to secure the original owner's name and location in order to contact them and perhaps solicit some assistance in regard to his cues and past training. The broker was unable to find the paperwork which would enable me to contact anyone regarding Cowboy's history. Imagine that. Okay, what to do next?

Realizing that I needed to locate a professional trainer for assistance, I readily scheduled a few riding sessions on site. The trainer was referred to me with high recommendations and was willing to work with Cowboy and me for as long as necessary in order for me to become the confident rider I needed to be—until the second lesson, at which time she informed me that Cowboy was definitely not a well-trained, settled, bomb-proof horse, and that she in fact would not even attempt to ride him herself, further stating,

> "You need to take this horse back where you got him and get your money back. He acts like a two-year-old."

I will never forget those words, nor my response which follows:

> "I can't take him back. He's part of my family now."

He was indeed a part of my family and owned a piece of my heart by that point in time, as he does to this day. But he has never since been ridden outside of an arena or round pen.

Lesson learned: I purchased the wrong horse for the right person. Hmmm…must run in the family.

The trainer was emphatic that this was not the right horse for me, but she did take pity on my situation, however, and continued to offer her services. I was, over a period of time, able to make *some* progress with him (riding him only in my round pen) and gained a more confident seat. In fact, she invited me to bring him to a professional horsemanship clinic on her farm for a weekend session, which I readily accepted. I was flattered that she perceived me as capable of handling Cowboy in an event setting with other horses and riders. She arranged for his transport, and I showed up bright and early on a beautiful Saturday morning full of expectations. Sadly, the weekend went downhill from that point forward.

The arena in which the event was to take place was a good distance from her barn. Most folks chose to ride their horses from barn to arena, but of course I knew better, so I walked Cowboy through the heavily wooded path. It became readily apparent that he suffered the same "studly" personality change whether under saddle or being led. I presented with a large hoof-shaped bruise on my right calf by the time I arrived at the arena. It seemed that he was deathly afraid of bushes.

This became even more apparent during our first trip around the inside of the arena, when he perceived a spectator seated on the ground outside the arena as a bear on attack, followed by yet another "attack bush" at the far end of the arena. By this time, he had evolved into a full gallop with absolutely no intention of stopping, bypassing all the other twenty plus riders. Meanwhile, the clinician was instructing me by microphone to "pull to the left, pull to the left!" Among God, me, and that clinician, Cowboy finally came to a stop, at which time I abruptly removed my shaking body from the saddle. I wasn't certain at that moment whether I would ever ride a horse again. I was petrified.

The clinician (a man) instructed me to remount. ("Are you kidding me?!") A woman would have recognized my impending tears and known I was not ready for this. I was obviously becoming his live training tool of the morning. I actually did make several efforts to remount at his request; however, Cowboy continued to walk away each time I placed my foot into the stirrup, further undermining my confidence. Finally, I refused to get back in the saddle. This clinician, who I will not mention by name, then proceeded to ridicule my timidity and fear, suggesting I remove myself and my horse to a nearby round pen where I spent the remainder of the entire weekend—alone. I felt like a first grader who had been remanded to the corner of the room. Tears, yes, there were a few. Regret, yes, there was regret at having spent *that* money for *that* weekend with *that* particular clinician. It was perhaps the worst $400 investment I ever made, and that's saying a lot. In fact, it actually set me back in my horsemanship skill and confidence level for quite some time.

Lesson learned: I took the wrong horse to the wrong event with the wrong clinician.

My next clinic I chose to audit rather than ride, becoming one of the blessed few to watch and learn at the hands of one of the nation's most acclaimed horsemen, Mr. Ray Hunt. In the not too distant past following this clinic, Mr. Hunt passed away, and I hope to see him again someday riding his horses through much greener pastures. He was an imposing and brusque clinician as well, however, and would likely have brought tears to my eyes had I been on horseback rather than merely auditing. He loved to bark commands at the riders, all the while pointing out their shortcomings. I recognize now that this was his "old cowboy way," and I would hopefully take it as such if ever again given the opportunity to do so.

Seize every opportunity to learn from the best.

Lessons to Be Learned

1.   Don't buy a horse from a broker unless you know and trust them, and even if you do, "buyer, beware!" Be sure you shovel through all that "sales muck" before you write that check. Bomb-proof and calm means *years* under saddle and sometimes an older horse is better than a younger one. If you need to build confidence as an older or inexperienced rider, don't buy a young horse. You never want to "learn how to ride together"! You want a horse who is an "old hand" at doing exactly what you expect him/her to do. The horse should help *you* with *your* training.

2.   Don't buy a horse compatible with someone else's riding skill level. Be honest with yourself in evaluating your personal skill level. A horse is only as good as its rider. As previously mentioned, the calm, well-behaved horse you see someone else ride can turn into a bucking bronco rodeo horse with a different rider. By the same token, a mature, well-trained, "dead broke" horse can make even

the most inexperienced riders look and feel accomplished and confident.

3. Don't purchase a horse for a "good deal." Again, bad choice. If a horse is "cheap" or a "good deal," there is usually a reason. Make the initial purchase a wise one. A little more money up front can sometimes mean a lot less money spent for training later on. A trainer or consultant who is not affiliated with a particular broker or breeder is worth every penny in providing you with an evaluation *before* you buy. For general riding needs, it is reasonable to spend from $100 to $300 or more for a consultation. You should, however, expect your consultant to make hands-on contact with your potential horse, working with the horse for a minimum of one to two hours as well as evaluating your personal riding skill level and goals.

4. Don't purchase a horse you have not ridden in a setting similar to the one in which you will be riding once you bring it home. Most definitely, do not purchase a horse which has not been used within and trained for the same horsemanship discipline for which you are intending to ride.

   Different horses are bred for differing "disciplines" or types of riding; that is, a dressage horse may not be suitable for trail riding, a cow penning horse is not what you would want as an endurance rider, and so forth.

   It is not possible to know if you are comfortable on a particular horse unless you actually ride that horse a few times. In my case, I never rode Cowboy outside an enclosed area; therefore, I did not recognize his tendencies to spook and strut until after I had brought him home and tried to ride him outside my pasture.

5. Don't purchase a horse because it's "pretty." Again, beauty is in the eye of the beholder, and when the beauty of the horse comes from within, just as with humans, it will

mark the beginning of a long and loving relationship. The prettiest horses on the outside can turn into absolute demons if you've not used good common sense and lots of horse sense before you make that purchase! "Blue eyes don't guarantee blue skies!"

6. Don't purchase a horse without having it vetted. A good equine vet will be honest and well worth the cost of an evaluation. They will be able to spot lameness, give you a good estimate of the horse's age, and evaluate overall state of health. It is not uncommon to have the previously established DVM for that particular horse provide you with this horse's health background. They are also a good source in regard to that horse's ground manners and behavior. How a horse behaves with its vet speaks volumes.

Lesson learned: Don't follow your heart without using your head.

Back to the barn. Cowboy's still there. *What do I do now?* I chose to continue on my quest for the best horse for me; at least, I had learned enough to know it was not Cowboy.

Enter Sunday Morning Surprise (a.k.a. Sunday), my Ultimate Best Horse for Life (UBHL). I had located another potential "perfect" horse for myself, in none other than the local *Carolina Bargain Trader* sales magazine. Searching out horses for sale, I saw an interesting listing for a gaited gelding, called the owner immediately, and scheduled an appointment to see if this horse could be my new UBHL.

Upon arriving at the appointment, I was introduced to a Peruvian Walking Horse attached to a $4500 price tag. This was a little out of my budget, but I had already figured out that a "cheap" horse was not likely to fulfill my personal needs. More training and time under saddle usually results in a higher cost.

My initial reaction to this particular horse was based upon his looks and his attitude—something about his demeanor made me uncomfortable—but the owner assured me that he was well-trained and a safe mount. I felt like less than a pro once I was in the saddle, and just to put it bluntly, I think our assessment of each other was mutual. He attempted to "rub me off" onto the arena fence several times, and not having been accustomed to gaited horses and their cues, I determined that he and I were not on the same wavelength. I managed to dismount with only a few bruises and a small scratch with minimal bleeding. (Not kidding!) The owner was extremely apologetic. In an effort to redirect her attention away from my battered ego (and legs!), I questioned her about a pretty little six-year-old Appaloosa/Saddlebred mare who was grazing with three or four other horses a few yards away, asking whether this horse might be available for sale. Naturally, I was once again attracted to the "pretty horse." (Some things never change!)

The horse about which I was asking belonged to their college-bound daughter and had tentatively been "promised" to a neighboring family. She was hesitant for me to ride that particular horse but finally agreed, since she was trying to fund upcoming college tuition. This horse, who they had nicknamed Miss Sue was six years old and had been born on their farm one early Sunday morning. Her birth by their newly purchased mare was completely unexpected; the owner's husband had seen the new filly darting down the barn aisle and had initially thought her to be a baby deer.

She (Miss Sue) allowed me to approach and saddle her. At first touch, I already felt as though we were old friends, and it only took a short ride for me to recognize the deep heart feeling one only experiences a few times in our lives with equines. I knew from that moment she would become my UBHL, and in fact, for years to come, I referred to her as my "perfect horse Sunday." Yes, I immediately changed her name to Sunday Morning Surprise, a name which suited her perfectly.

Although it took several days and a few consultations with my trainer, I finally brought my Sunday Girl to her new "forever home." The owner reluctantly agreed to let her go and has on several occasions tried to buy her back; she knew what a good horse Sunday had become. I felt a bit of a conscience attack whenever she called because I knew they had thought of Sunday as a family member, but the attack didn't last long whenever I recalled the initial name they had given her and recognized that they didn't perceive her as I did—the fulfillment of every little girl's dream horse. She is, and if God allows, will always be my Sunday Morning Surprise. Sort of like that Christmas Morning Surprise I always dreamt about!

In Sunday's case, I did pay more for her than is generally acceptable for an unregistered horse in this area—$3000—but she was worth every cent. I applied most of the "common sense" rules I had learned from my experience with Cowboy:

1. I did not purchase her from a broker, but rather from her original owners. Therefore, I felt I had most of her background and training information.
2. I was advised by them that she had been ridden by children and adults, as well as shown in several 4-H events. In fact, she had been frequently ridden on mountain trails, and had actually been used as a bride's mount for a mountaintop wedding in Black Mountain, North Carolina. Her initial training for basic riding development was done by a local professional trainer, and she responded to verbal cues as well as more subtle leg cues.
3. Once I had ridden her, but prior to bringing her to our farm, the previous owner had already agreed to allow me a two-week time frame within which I could have her vetted and work with her adequately to know that I had made the right choice in buying her.

I did follow my heart, but I used my head as well. There was much prayer involved for me in making this decision, and I know the Lord provided the answer.

"Delight thyself also in the Lord; and He shall give thee the desires of
thine heart"

Psalm 37:4, kjv

Lesson learned and applied—finally!

Don't Expect Help and Encouragement from Your Family or Friends

At some point during that first year of horse ownership, I realized that my horses had become a bit of a full-time project. Although I had initially expected my family to become a part of this new (yet old) passion of mine, it was apparent that no one else in the family, with the exception of my wheelchair-bound dad, seemed to share that true passion. Furthermore, no one was interested in investing their time into anything beyond a few moments on occasion to ride an already fully groomed and saddled horse— saddled and groomed by me, of course, since anything else would have required one to dirty their hands and clothes with horse dirt and sweat!

In fact, whenever the subject of horses was mentioned within close friend and family circles, it only served as fuel to the fires of discontent and dissatisfaction of my then-husband, who resented the time and particularly the money expended toward any and all things equine. I quickly learned to steer clear of horse-related discussions other than with fellow horse enthusiasts.

In my effort to stimulate a bit of horse enthusiasm within my young granddaughters, I attempted a few riding lessons with them and journeyed out on another "horse quest" to find a special horse for them to call their own. I did in fact purchase two additional horses, employing all my previously learned lessons, hoping to generate the same type of equine passion that I had always enjoyed. I had failed to consider their already busy school schedule, however, and it became painfully obvious within a very short period of time that their interest in horses was primarily directed toward those of the stuffed and photographed variety. Although the youngest of my three granddaughters and more recently my two young grandsons do share my equine interest to a somewhat lesser degree, the objectionable combination of extreme heat and cold, gnats, flies, and manure have managed to deter any hands-on participation from most of my remaining adult family members. What a disappointment for me! By the point in time at which I recognized that they had not inherited the "horse gene," I had managed to invest several thousand dollars in an effort to find that perfect horse for them as well.

In spite of the brutal realization that my family as a whole was not interested in sharing my horse-related chores and responsibilities, the time I spent with Sunday and Cowboy over the next several months were eventful, fulfilling, and therapeutic. However, as in most challenges which require knowledge and experience, we recognize that the more we learn, the more there is to be learned. Horses and all things equine are highly representative of this theory. A few of those previously heretofore unknown facts included but were most certainly not limited to:

1. Horses should be eyeballed for soundness at least once or twice daily. If a horse is lame or has other health issues, the time lost before calling your vet for advice cannot be recovered, and you can easily lose your horse to permanent disability or even death.

2. Horses drink an average of eleven to fifteen gallons of water daily. They prefer water above fifty-five degrees Fahrenheit, and on hot summer days, more readily drink cool water as opposed to water that has been warmed too much by the sun. Access to water is required in order to prevent colic.

3. Colic—ah yes, colic! Prior to having my first horse as an adult, my only exposure to colic was from my infant

son, and babies, unlike horses, generally do not die from colic. In our equine friends, colic is a description of the horse's gut having lost its natural ability to pass food along the intestinal canal. It can be brought on by a number of things, including but not limited to: inadequate water, insufficient forage, sudden changes in feed product and presentation, severe and unusual weather patterns (yes, particularly the onslaught of a drop in temperature with ice and rain), or basically any type of extreme stress to the horse's system, to mention just a few.

4. Regular stall cleaning is mandatory. An average horse produces approximately eight thousand pounds of manure per year. I currently have ten horses on my farm, which equates to eighty thousand pounds of manure annually. I found this to be astounding, and even more so was the fact that some horses prefer to poop only in their stall, even when they are provided acres of pasture. Cowboy was one of those horses initially, and it seemed apparent to me that he politely waited for me to finish his stall cleaning and distribution of fresh wood shavings, after which he would presumably "mark" his stall with manure almost immediately. In fact, he also acquired the unique ability to "target" his wall-mounted feed bucket with manure, and I eventually had to remove it from his stall.

5. Feeding routines are normally quite rigid due to the previously mentioned tendency toward colic; and where there are two or more horse owners, trainers, vets, or feed distributors together, there will be no shortage or opinions as to which brand and method of feeding is recommended. There is, however, one rule of thumb on which all will agree:

Maintain a consistent type of feed and feeding routine; make any changes to that routine gradually!

Domesticated horses are only distant relatives of those free-roaming horses we have all seen roaming the western United States in those old cowboy movies we watched as young children. The domesticated horse will eat and enjoy a number of free-growing plants and shrubs which are highly toxic. In addition, if allowed free access to their grains and feed, they will literally eat until they kill themselves. Lock up your feed, folks! Become an expert on all your locally grown plants, trees, and shrubs if you don't wish to lose your new best friend to colic. I have always understood that one must childproof a home prior to having a roaming toddler in the house; little did I know until my adult equine experience that one also has to detoxify their entire pasture and adjacent fence-line areas, not to mention horse-proofing all grain and feed supplements.

As referenced earlier, the more I learned regarding the upkeep and daily rituals required in order to maintain healthy, well-balanced horses, the more I recognized the enormity of the task at hand. In retrospect, I should have limited the size of my "little" herd to accommodate my personal enjoyment in order for me to reap more productive riding and training time. The horses that ultimately made their way to our little farm have all become a part of my equine family, but the family time I had envisioned with my grandchildren riding trails, camping, and attending horse events failed to develop.

Do not presume that your own interests permeate to your family, and do not invest in a horse for someone else until and unless you absolutely recognize in that person the actual passion for horses you wish them to have!

Lessons to Be Learned

1. If your child, grandchild, or even your spouse expresses an interest in wanting a horse of their own, wait! Investigate local opportunities for them to be exposed to horses and horse events, including an extended period of riding lessons with a good instructor. A few weeks of lessons are not adequate to be objective in determining whether your child has a true passion for all things horse and horse-related.

2. In selecting an instructor for these lessons, be certain that your child is required to perform and follow through with all things pertaining to the grooming, riding, tacking, feeding, and upkeep of an equine. This most definitely should include stall cleaning. Your child should be expected to maintain a "horse routine" over a period of months which include a variety of weather patterns. Those chores which may seem minimal during nice weather can become insurmountable during ice and snow. Horse ownership is a 365-days-per-year, and on occasion a 24-hours-a-day, responsibility.

3. Allow your child to be involved in determining the direction of horse discipline which interests *them*. Although your interest may lie within dressage, their interest may be more toward Western pleasure or trail riding. You should also note that one discipline does not necessarily preclude another, and it is likely that the child's interests will expand and perhaps evolve from one to another as their age and ability progresses. It should be noted that many horses are able to "cross over" as well; that is, it is now a commonly accepted practice for a dressage or show horse to cross over into trail riding, and many trainers recognize that the trail riding aspect ultimately exposes the horse to

obstacles and learning experiences that will benefit them in the show ring.

4. Once you have determined that your child shows promise toward true horse passion, consider a horse lease option. Many barns have horses that they can lease to you for a period of time rather than your having to be initially responsible for the complete ownership and housing of a horse. In some cases, one may be able to share a lease with another party, thereby further reducing your costs. However, each barn will offer different lease options and it is essential that you understand and fully communicate, in writing, exactly what the lease conditions are. Essentially, a lease option will allow you and your child to experience the pleasures and responsibilities of horse ownership without your having to make an initial permanent obligation.

By adhering to these prescribed activities over a significant period of time, should you deem that you and your child are truly ready to experience horse ownership, you will be prepared, informed, and willing to wait for the right horse—the horse who will become your UBHL.

Note: I feel impressed to say that my granddaughters never actually asked me to buy a horse for them. This was something I did of my own accord, and I take full responsibility for trying to direct their interest toward horses. My two young grandsons now live on the farm, and although they currently do express a desire to be involved with our horses, my goal is to allow them to experience both the responsibilities as well as the enjoyment of equine ownership, understanding that as they grow older their interests are subject to change. A few years of feeding, watering, and cleaning stalls during inclement weather will provide an indicator. Only time will tell...

Again, lesson learned.

Section 2
Farm Photos

Horse Life in Action - Common Sense Applied

Cowboy and Those Beautiful Sky Blue Eyes

This is where it all began, but it's easy to
see why I fell in love with him!

Daily Line-Up

The natural pecking order of this little herd can be witnessed in this photograph. This photo was taken as grain was being prepared, and the actual pecking order of the herd is according to their place in line. Cowboy is first, followed by Twinkle (who although small, established her seniority on the farm early on); next in line is Sunday, who generally does take the "middle child" position in whichever herd she is placed; following in the rear is Lady Bug (who has now passed on) and represents the older, more feeble horse. The pecking order is generally determined based upon which horse has the ability to be in charge of the other horses; this position changes regularly based upon size, age, seniority, and sometimes orneriness! It is imperative for the human to reestablish their own position daily.

Our First Baby

Dwight gets up close and personal at dawn's first light with newly born colt Midnight, Gentle Spirit's first foal. It's important to "handle" and expose a new foal to as many sounds, touches, and smells as possible during the first few hours after birth. This process is known as *imprinting*. This familiarization will enhance later training experiences for both the horse and the trainer.

Midnight and Michaela

Midnight and Michaela are getting to know one another. He is wearing a foal halter, which familiarizes him with the sensation of being haltered, and Michaela is allowing him time to become acquainted with her as well as to the brush before grooming begins.

Baby, It's Cold Outside!

Midnight and I are both ready for winter in our heavy
winter coats! By allowing Midnight to gradually adapt
to cold temperatures without the use of *blanketing*,
he has naturally grown adequate "fur" to keep him
warm and toasty. He is only eight months old here
and is very people oriented. I have to routinely remind
him to stay out of my personal space unless invited!

Round Pen Work

Regular on-line ground work with Midnight is essential in order for him to learn the respect, cues, balance, and self-control which is required and expected of him whether under saddle or at liberty. Notice the loose rein and my hand position, which indicates that he is responding to the feel of the halter and rope, as well as to my personal calm energy level rather than to force.

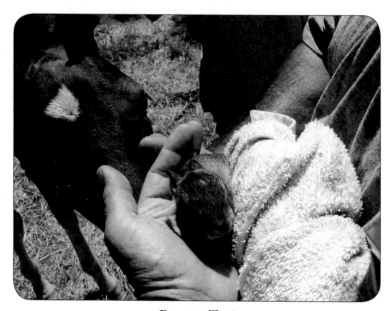

Bunnies Too!

There's more to life on the farm than horses—such as the rescue of a baby bunny whose home was disrupted by the tractor while mowing pastures. Miracle looks on while Dwight and I examine the bunny for injuries.

Somebody's Gotta Do It!

Stall cleaning, grass cutting, training sessions, horse grooming, and other feeding and farm chores leave little time for pleasure riding! However, the satisfaction of being able to work with horses feeds my equine passion while I attempt to earn a future profit in return. "Do something you love for a living and you'll never have to work a day in your life."

What to Ride Today?

Horse-keeping is not limited to riding horses; I have to wear my tractor and mower-riding hat more often than my riding helmet! Retirement is not an option for a rancher or a farmer, and there is no such thing as "weekends off."

Our Special Farm Princess

DD was born to Cool Skippin' Lizzy and is shown here at first morning light being greeted by Lacey and Trigger, who shared the adjoining paddock. Dwight is making himself available to monitor this first interaction, assuring that no aggressive behavior is permitted. DD was born quite unfortunately and unexpectedly with HYPP, a genetic problem which ultimately ended her life here with us just prior to her second birthday. She was full of personality and was *born* an alpha mare! She brought much joy to the farm, and will always remain alive in our hearts; she rests in our family cemetery here at Gentle Spirit Resting Place.

DD Prancing Around!

At only a few weeks old, she was full of energy and fun, serving as a living educational tool for all the horse enthusiasts who visited the farm, both old and young alike.

After a "Night on the Town"

This photo was taken early one morning when I looked out my back door and realized DD had managed to get out of her paddock, and had been leisurely strolling around the various pastures all night, now opting for a brief rest in my back yard. As you can see, she knows she "owns the place." Although this is one of my favorite photos of her, it brings about a sense of melancholy, as it serves to remind me that life is beautiful and precious—but fleeting. DD passed away within a few short weeks after this photo was taken. Life with horses—and humans—is not always full of happiness. But it is our choice whether to focus on the joy or the sorrow.

Learning to be Patient

At each horse's feeding time, I take the opportunity to reestablish my position as the leader within each herd. Here I am with Nikki Two-Eyes, our "rescue horse," requiring her to walk, stop, and back up before approaching her feeding bunker. Nikki was previously food-deprived, and the training opportunity of having her be patient prior to feeding, although difficult for her, enables her to remain calm and submissive, recognizing me as her leader on a daily basis.

The Proper Approach

Michaela is shown here approaching her horse, Babe, at one of the kids' horse camps offered at Gentle Spirit Stables several years ago. She is properly holding the lead rope and is mentally prepared to gently lay it across Babe's neck. Babe is aware of her approach and is expecting to be haltered.

Allowing Babe to Accept Grooming

In this recent photo, Michaela is allowing Babe to both see and smell the curry brush prior to grooming. This is a trust-building ritual and is appropriate before the use of any grooming tool or application of medicine, tools, or tack.

Trust

It is notable in this photo that Babe is standing with a relaxed frame of mind while Michaela is grooming, although she is neither tied nor haltered. This is reflective of complete trust on the part of both human and horse.

Relationship Demonstrated

The relationship that can be established between human and horse is evident in this photo as well. Babe, by nature, is not trusting of most humans in general, but Michaela has, through consistency and confidence, built a strong, trusting relationship with her that has and will continue to endure throughout a lifetime. It should be noted that Michaela, much like Babe, is not particularly generous with her own sense of trust, and reserves her genuine smiles for occasions such as this. *There's nothing quite like a girl and her horse.*

Our New Barn Baby

My UBHL, Sunday, nuzzles her new filly, Miracle, after an early morning Father's Day birth. Although we were there to assist when necessary, Sunday knew by instinct exactly what to do once her new baby was born. We had anticipated and prepared for this birth for weeks, and Dwight's facial expression suggests that this is a great Father's Day gift. Miracle was our third Gentle Spirit baby (sired unexpectedly by then two-year-old Midnight), and as can be seen in the photograph, we had prepared a beautiful paddock and stall covered with hay for a suitable bed. We added 2 × 4 boards underneath the fence panels to prevent the possibility of the tiny foal rolling underneath.

Like Mother, Like Daughter

As can be seen here, a young filly or colt will stay close to mom until weaning time, closely imitating the mare's behavior and attitude. It is important to expose a young horse to "barn buddies" who reflect calm and gentle personalities; your horse will tend to mimic the conduct of those horses with whom they bond.

Early Learning

As Sunday and Miracle leisurely eat grain from their low feeding bunker, I am taking the opportunity to lift Miracle's feet. By doing so, I am allowing her to associate her foot being lifted and cleaned with the pleasant sensation of eating. I also used a similar routine to help her comply with haltering; I offered daily grain in her bucket while holding her halter in such a fashion as to require the placement of her mouth through the halter in order to access her grain.

Imprinting Established

As a result of proper "imprinting" at birth, Miracle easily accepts most procedures such as deworming (shown here), immunizations, hoof trimming, grooming, etc. In general, she trusts the human not to impose harm upon her, and is usually more curious regarding new objects rather than frightened.

Granmommy's Helpers

My grandsons, Gavin and Noah, like nothing better than to help prepare buckets for feeding, carefully measuring out each horse's portion with their vitamins, minerals, joint formula,
and garlic. They understand that "horses love
grain," but that it must be limited to prevent colic.

It's a Family Thing

Gavin is already adept at filling the water buckets in all five pastures. His assistance is much appreciated, especially on those days when time is running short and I need another pair of hands. Horse-keeping is a family affair and a big responsibility.

Little Hand, Big Heart

Horses have big hearts, and they will almost certainly respond to the little hand of a child reaching out to them. Miracle and Noah are becoming well acquainted, and Noah's confidence and calm demeanor is reflected back to him as Miracle welcomes his friendly touch.

The Natural Way

Gavin has already learned that horses respond better when they are allowed to respond to our requests, rather than being forced. Walking on a loose rein as opposed to being pulled and tugged transcends into a more cooperative attitude and ultimately leads toward the trust and relationship necessary for an enjoyable experience for both the horse and human. An understanding of the horse's natural instincts as an animal of prey is implemented in the practice of natural horsemanship, enabling the training of both horse and human to progress efficiently.

Just the Right Size

Twinkle is happy to cooperate and just the right size for a child—in this case Gavin—to learn the art of hoof cleaning. Riding lessons should always include grooming, tacking up the horse, and barn chores.

Treats, Anyone?

Noah has proclaimed in no uncertain terms that Twinkle is *his* horse! Although he is not yet quite old enough to benefit from structured riding lessons, he knows how to hold his hand properly while offering treats, and is always ready for a brief ride whenever one is offered. Little by little, he is gaining equine knowledge and confidence through his daily exposure to the horse-keeping rituals here on the farm where he resides, and when he is a little older, lessons will be offered to him if he is interested and willing.

Horse Trainer in the Making?

Only time will tell whether Gavin's equine interests will continue into adulthood, but he definitely has all the correct ingredients at his disposal. At the very least, his interaction with the horses here will provide confidence-building and lend itself toward the development of a good work ethic and a responsible nature.

Green Pastures

Cowboy and Twinkle are the two horses who launched my personal life with horses as an adult. This photo exemplifies good-quality forage and my personal preference for horse shelter, a three-sided run-in. This run-in shelter offers easy entrance and exit, providing shade and inclement weather protection, but just as importantly allows the horse to use the shelter at will. As a result, I generally do not have to deal with an overly energetic horse who has been confined within a stall for long periods of time.

All the Pretty Horses

Okay, I will admit it. This is me at the end of the day enjoying my "sweet horse life," and like I've said before, "There's nothing quite like a girl and her horse. And for some girls, it takes more than one!" P.S. I would like to point out how smart Miracle is; she is shown in this photo trying to figure out how to break the string on the bale of hay by using her front hoof. Makes a grandma proud!

Section 3
Your Horse Dream

So Now You're Ready to Buy Your Horse

Okay, so you've read about some of the mistakes made during my personal horse quest, as well as a few of my childhood horse experiences. Hopefully you have taken to heart these hard-earned lessons and will go forward with a new sense of enlightenment and determination to avoid some of these pitfalls.

My personal goal for you as the reader is twofold:

1. That you will learn from my experience and the common mistakes which could have been avoided
2. That you have already made the wise decision to use head knowledge rather than heart emotions as you continue in the pursuit of your own personal horse quest

You're ready to fulfill those childhood dreams of horse ownership and need some actual direction. By taking a business-like approach toward the fulfillment of your decision, you should apply the following guidelines as closely as possible.

1. *Which Horse Discipline*: As you know, you must first decide toward which horse discipline your interests are best suited. In order to best evaluate this, I would suggest you visit as many local horse events, barns, and shows as possible. By doing so, you will be able to immediately develop a personal feel or interest and can observe some of the physical as well as training requirements necessary in each of the varying disciplines.

For instance, an older rider may not be physically able to achieve and remain safe in a discipline such as reining or jumping. On the other hand, you may already know that you prefer the look of Western riding as opposed to English or dressage. Again, one does not necessarily preclude the other, but your initial pursuit of the best horse for you should be directed toward one which has been predominantly trained and used for the discipline in which you are most interested.

Here are a few possibilities to consider:

    a. English or Western
    b. Pleasure riding or showing
    c. Endurance competition or trail or both
    d. Reining
    e. Cow penning
    f. Huntseat or dressage
    g. None of the above

2. *Which Breed*: The breed of the horse you select will most definitely need to be suited toward your personal riding interest. It is imperative that you familiarize yourself with a variety of breeds, particularly the aspects of that breed's temperament as well as physical characteristics. The height and size of a horse is relevant to you as a rider and your ability to comfortably mount and ride that particular breed. Different breeds of horses have a different feel to their ride due to their overall build and musculature. In addition, horse temperament is also affected by its breed and direct bloodlines. A Thoroughbred is not likely to be a suitable choice for a young or inexperienced rider; a Quarter Horse bred for reining is not likely the best choice for someone interested in the pursuit of dressage.

I would suggest you do research regarding the various breeds available; a combination of written horse encyclopedias as well as Internet access is helpful. Just remember that most Internet sites promoting a particular breed are also likely trying to sell that breed. An objective viewpoint is required when you approach this process.

3. *Sources of Information:* Check out and explore various training methods. The RFD-TV network offers a variety of equine-related shows, including several internationally renowned trainers and clinicians. By viewing a number of these clinicians, you will be able to determine the direction and techniques most likely to suit your personal comfort level. When you are evaluating a particular horse, as well as pursuing a personal horse trainer and/or consultant, your understanding of these various techniques is mandatory in making the selection toward which you will ultimately be suited.

   You will notice that trainers and clinicians vary with their methods primarily as they relate to their own temperament and nature. Similar to different parenting techniques, trainers tend to display either a strict line in their training technique or a more relationship-oriented approach. Happily, there are also those who fall somewhere in the middle, which I have found to be more in line with my own personal comfort level.

   It is imperative that you evaluate an adequate number of training methods prior to engaging a personal trainer, and also apply this understanding in order to search out a horse which has been trained using similar techniques. Ultimately, this will limit excessive training for both you and your horse in the future.

4. *To Board or to Build:* Whether to house your horse elsewhere or to build a suitable stable and pasture on site is more than a budget decision; it is potentially life-

changing and is worthy of careful evaluation. There are a number of things that should be considered, with both pros and cons on either side of the equation.

Boarding pros include the following:
Stall cleaning, regular feeding, and general horse health requirements and accommodations are provided by someone other than yourself. *This is especially appealing if you have work responsibilities, or if you like to travel and go on vacations.* You will always be comfortable with the knowledge that a competent horse lover is taking care of your new UBHL. In addition, most barns will accommodate your needs pertaining to hoof care and vet checks. Most boarding facilities provide round pen areas as well as arenas and accessibility to trails; in most cases, transportation services are offered when necessary.

Boarding cons may include the following:
Boarding fees can be pricey, and many services are considered as "add-ons"; some of these fees may apply to holding your horse for vet checks and hoof care services, equine transportation, blanketing services, unusual feed routines, etc. These extra services should be addressed within the boarding contract.

Other considerations will be the exposure and interaction of your horse with other horses on the property, as well as other boarders and hired help. In all herds (*herd* is defined as a group of two or more horses) there will always be an alpha horse, and there will always be a distinguishable pecking order. In some cases this is reestablished throughout the day and is ongoing. What this can mean for you will depend on whether your horse is compliant within the herd. Horses are somewhat like human beings in that they tend to pick up bad habits from others. In addition, there is always risk of injury from other horses within a herd. Biting, ear pinning, and kicking are common, and if you are going to be a nervous wreck every time you leave your horse, then integrated boarding is likely *not* going to be the best direction for you.

So you've decided to board:

Should you determine that boarding is the best solution for you and your horse, it is mandatory that you investigate all the potential barns in your area, visiting them on a variety of occasions without an appointment. Your observations of the horse behavior there, the barn and stall conditions, and whether there is anyone on site taking care of the animals will give you a good indication of whether it is a suitable location for you and your horse. In addition, you should question boarders at each location, soliciting their opinion of the facility and getting an indication of their satisfaction.

Interview the barn manager and do not hesitate to ask any questions, whether they seem trivial or not. Have them explain their normal daily routines, including but not limited to stall cleaning procedures, feeding products and routines, exercise and turnout routine, making certain to clarify the responsibilities which they deem yours as well as theirs. Inquire regarding all rules, add-on fees, and accessibility to round pens, arenas, and trails. It is also important to determine whether they will permit your personal trainer to work with you and your horse at their facility, especially if they already have a trainer on site. Verify whether you need to reserve your round pen and arena usage and how many hours are allowed. Be certain, as I have previously mentioned, to inquire regarding the type of horsemanship training they are accustomed to at that barn. If, during this interview process, you intuitively feel that the two of you do not experience significant commonalities pertaining to horses and horsemanship, do not hesitate to look elsewhere. Better to recognize this prior to getting your horse settled into an environment which you will find unsuitable and stressful. Life with your new UBHL should not be stressful; it should be therapeutic and relaxing!

All right—so you like the facility, you love the barn manager, you "click" with the boarders you chatted up. You're ready to make a boarding commitment—but *read the fine print first!* Ask for a copy of the boarding contract and take it home. Read it at home, and then read it a second and third time; make sure you understand the legalities and recognize that you do have the option of appending the contract to include any items which you deem necessary. In some instances, you may even wish to secure a legal opinion, depending on the situation. Just make certain that you are completely satisfied with the agreement you are making *before* you actually proceed! Keep in mind, however, that life is not predictable and you are dealing with an animal which is prone to colic, mischief, and injury (horses as well as human!); it is impossible to include all potential scenarios.

Building Pros:

Keeping your horse on site or near your home is enticing to most folks for a number of reasons. The concept of going out to the barn for a short grooming visit or a brief training session and the general knowledge of having your horse nearby are satisfying. Having your own barn and pasture enables you to interact with and enjoy your horse throughout the day. It is reassuring to know that your horse is receiving your personally supervised training, care, and attention, something which is akin to home schooling your child. Building your own barn and riding areas will allow you to design and build-in your own personal touches according to your needs, whether they be grandiose or minimal.

For most people, the acreage available for pasture is their first consideration, understanding that *a minimum of two acres per horse* is recommended, with additional pasture acreage optimal. Hand in hand with available pasture needs are budget considerations. If you are equipped with adequate pasture area and comfortable with your budget to build and maintain your premises, then it is important for you to be aware of the potential negative considerations as well.

Building Cons:

Some considerations which should be taken seriously prior to building include, but are not limited to, the following:

Although it is extremely satisfying to have your new horse at your disposal throughout the day, the responsibility of caring for your horse will likely rest solely upon your shoulders unless you are blessed with the financial ability to hire a full-time barn manager. This includes feeding, stall cleaning, and manure disposal/disbursement, grooming, daily handling and exercise requirements, etc. You will need to be available for regular hoof trimming appointments and vetting, which generally occur during the normal workweek rather than on weekends. Someone must be available 365 days a year, and on occasion twenty-four hours a day, to maintain and care for your horse's needs. This is significant in that it most definitely will impact your life in regard to vacations and spontaneity; you have to plan in advance for horse care much as you would plan to care for a small child or an aging adult parent. I believe the responsibility factor to be the biggest consideration one needs to make in determining whether to board or to build. It can most definitely impact your life in a negative direction, depending on your individual circumstances. In order to maintain harmony in your home, this must be a mutual decision to be discussed and agreed upon by all those who will be affected.

Okay. So everyone is in agreement, the kids are excited, your spouse is willing to pitch in, you have extra help lined up and you're ready to build. How big and how much is it going to cost? Whatever amount you ultimately determine after getting your building bids and equipment needs estimated, *double that figure.* Everything will cost more than you anticipate, especially when you are building to suit a horse's needs. In your excitement at the prospect of having your new UBHL within arm's reach, your mind will hear the lower estimates and rationalize about the final cost factors, but in reality the final budget should reflect the highest estimates and potential costs. Otherwise, by the time your project is complete and you are ready to bring your new horse baby home, you will be stressed and guilt-ridden due to the actual amount of money you have had to invest. Do not allow this to happen to you; the experience of bringing your new dream horse home and fulfilling your once-in-a-lifetime dream should not be overshadowed by anxiety and guilt. Plan for your expenses and use real figures!

Building a budget—big or small:

Except for a very lucky few, the budget has to be considered, and if you are reading this book regarding "common sense" as it pertains to horse-keeping, you're likely not one of those lucky few. It is easy to fall prey to all those books and pamphlets that describe elaborate barns and pastures. After all, those are the ones we see in movies, television, and in most equine-related educational books. However, that is where your common sense comes into play. I have, myself, on more than one occasion, drawn out and considered plans for elaborate, and some not-so-elaborate barns, pastures, and covered arenas. Most of us have visited several horse centers and witnessed the convenience of grandiose stalls, inlaid-brick barn aisles, perfectly raked enclosed riding arenas, and lush, perfectly manicured pastures.

Consider *yourself* one of the "lucky few" now as I tell you, "Those expensive elaborate buildings and stalls are not necessary for the health and happiness of your horse." These lovely amenities serve the purpose of the human rather than the equine. In and of themselves, they create in most cases a more convenient and protected environment for the *human*. Your horse does not require, need, appreciate, and—in most circumstances—does not even prefer these amenities!

Think about horses in general. Left to their own devices and given their own choices, they huddle together in the pasture during most storms, including rain and snow. They go into their confined stall areas for only four basic needs: feeding, shade, occasional shelter, and to poop. Otherwise, they live completely outside of their stalls, spending the remainder of their day grazing, sunning themselves, napping, and occasionally getting a little exercise on their own. If the weather is extreme, either hot or cold, they seek out shelter; and in most cases, a run-in shed will be their choice rather than an enclosed stall. As an example, I personally observed my horses just yesterday during an extreme summer storm with heavy rain and brisk wind. Only two of eleven horses chose to go inside their shelter; the other nine seemed perfectly content to huddle over their hay with head down and foot cocked in a resting position, patiently waiting for the storm to pass.

Wild horses have been observed for hundreds of years as they roam the ranges, and never once have I seen recorded an episode of a horse who sought out a small dark cave in which to live. Enclosed stalls were created and continue to be used for the convenience and vanity (yes, I said "vanity") of the human. We stall our horses almost exclusively to prevent grooming issues such as sun bleaching, cleanliness (per our human standards), scrapes and scratches, and last but not least, the ability to easily "catch and halter" at our convenience.

My personal concept of a more "natural horsemanship" method of horse-keeping is to allow the horse more freedom to live as nature intended, thereby creating a satisfied, calm, happy, and more mentally stable horse. In order to accomplish this goal, I have recognized that my personal little herd requires only the following:

a. Pasture for grazing, with approximately one to two acres per horse
b. Run-in stalls to accommodate the number of horses in that particular paddock

c. Several small gated areas in the paddock, enabling segregation of horses when necessary; that is, confinement during illness, birthing, or when introducing new horses into the herd, as well as during their daily feeding routine

d. Fresh watering access absolutely required and electrical access if possible

I have determined that my cash is far better spent toward the provision of quality forage and feed, a suitable fencing and gate system, and heavy-duty, three-sided run-in sheds, which require minimal maintenance.

5. *Other Budget Considerations*:

Vetting:

It goes without saying that a dependable equine vet is mandatory, and the cost of vetting most definitely needs to be determined when considering your budget. I have used a variety of vets over the course of my life with horses, including large animal vets and equine specialists. My personal experience with the large animal vet who I used for several years resulted in the death of a new foal and the near-death of a prized mare. I found this particular vet to be compassionate and well-intentioned, but far less knowledgeable in regard to my horses, in comparison to the equine specialist who I now use and have come to love as my new friend. In contrast to the large animal vet, my current equine vet, Karen M. Bullock, DVM, has worked exclusively with horses during most of her entire career and quite naturally has been exposed to most potential equine disease, injury, and illness. Her horse handling experience is evident during farm calls, and she recognizes those instances where her immediate presence is necessary. She never hesitates to offer suggestions and is most agreeable to my handling as many medical applications as possible on my own. I am extremely blessed to have found her.

Seek out the best, not the cheapest.

"'I always thank God for you.'"

1 Corinthians 1:4, niv

Forage and Fresh Water:

Your horse cannot survive without good-quality forage and an adequate supply of fresh water. The type of hay you choose will depend upon the area in which you live as well as recommendations by your equine vet and local area horse owners. There are many considerations when determining which hay is best for your particular horse. Some choices may include Coastal Bermuda, Timothy, Alfalfa, Orchard Grass, etc. There is a vast difference in cost from one to the other, with Coastal Bermuda being the most economical in my area of residence. It should be noted that shredded or pelleted beet pulp as well as stabilized rice bran are invaluable forage sources and can be used to supplement your hay.

The variety of hay you use will determine what types of feed and supplements are necessary, and a horse's purpose and activity level will impact this decision as well. As an example, in my particular situation, I strictly use Coastal Bermuda hay supplemented with a vitamin and mineral product plus a minimal amount of easily digestible pelleted feed. (Note: I will discuss my personal feed choices in more detail later.) In addition, I have established Bermuda grass pastures during the spring and summer months.

It is imperative that you determine the most easily accessible hay in your area, as well as its cost. Horses cannot always be easily switched from one type of hay to the other; any change in forage or feed must be accomplished on a gradual basis in order to avoid colic. Therefore, it is essential to locate a good-quality hay source and to discuss the type of hay recommended by your vet; the prior owner of your horse should advise you as to which types of feed and forage have been used in the past.

Feed:

There are almost as many feed types and brands as there are folks who will give you their personal opinion on such. Having said that, I will express *my* thoughts and choices to you, using my own experience and applying my "common sense" method to the equation.

Initially, after bringing home my first UBHL (or so I thought at the time), namely, Cowboy, I applied all the traditional feeding methods and routines offered up by my local feed dealer and other horse folks in my area. I used a popular and well-advertised brand of feed, feeding according to the horse's weight and usage as prescribed by the feed company. Cowboy was and continues to be what is known in the horse world as an "easy keeper." And that's a good thing! His body weight is easy to maintain, and he does not require any specialty feeds or types of hay.

At one point, however, I did defer to the advice of another local horse owner who suggested a more specialized feed that was intended to be a broad spectrum and healthier product. It didn't take more than a week or two to determine that it essentially made him a little "crazy"! Another term which I learned during that period was the term *hot*, as in "crazy horse." Not a great thing for me! ("Hot" is to horses as "high-strung" is to humans.) This feed included high protein ingredients that Cowboy did not need. It probably made him feel a little more excitable and energetic, but it certainly did not make him safe to ride. Perhaps if we were engaged in barrel racing or endurance riding, this higher energy feed would have been appropriate.

Lesson to be learned: The type of feed product should be in line with the type of activity level (discipline), age, and breed of the horse.

Following my experience with the high energy feed, I went back to the 10 percent pelleted feed, which I had previously used and continued to use until I had several other horses in my care who were older and most of whom were *not* considered "easy keepers." At that point in time, my feed struggle began anew; I found myself purchasing several different types of feed and preparing various combinations of feed and feed supplements. More horses will always require more complexity in feed rituals; as a result, I was constantly seeking a simpler and more common sense method of feeding. My husband (Yes, I remarried!) refused to help me feed during this time because he insisted that it was too complicated. In retrospect, I was using four different feeds with additional supplements for my little herd in order to provide for the easy keepers, the older horses, the brood mares, the yearlings, and one horse with HYPP, whose potassium level must be limited. It was quite a challenge to prepare each bucket and even more challenging to engage someone who I believed to be competent to feed for me in order to have a day away from the farm.

"I needed something simpler!"

God did again recognize the desires of my heart, and he must have directed my path to a Clinton Anderson Tour Stop Event, where I was introduced to ADM Alliance Nutrition feed products. "Thank you, Lord!"

During this event, I attended a seminar hosted by ADM Alliance Nutrition and recognized that their approach to equine feed production was truly the answer for me and my little herd of horses. Their product is forage-based, and by using a combination of their stabilized rice bran Senior feed with one to two ounces of their vitamin and mineral additive, I can feed all my horses in essentially the same manner. In fact, as long as I provide continual good-quality hay for grazing and access to their ADM vitamin/mineral blocks, my "graining" requirement is only necessary in order for them to maintain a healthy weight.

It should be noted that ADM Alliance Nutrition does not necessarily endorse my personal feeding routine; each bag, of course, provides feeding instructions as they pertain to the individual horse's body weight, age, and body condition, as well as performance expectations. I supplement my hay (together with an ADM vitamin/mineral block) with pelleted feed primarily when adequate forage is not available.

In my particular circumstance, I believe keeping it simple is keeping it best. My horses are happy and they are healthy. Just as importantly, I am happy, I am healthy, and I am not stressed out over their feeding routines anymore! The vet says our horses look great; my hoof care expert (who, by the way has also switched her horses to ADM Alliance Nutrition) says their feet have never looked better, and I can leave them in someone else's care for a day or two without stressing out over their feed routine! The so-called proof in the pudding is that not one of the ten horses in my care have had colic for the more than three-year period since I have been using ADM equine feed.

An additional benefit in using this feed is that my feed cost decreased by approximately $1000 (for ten horses) per year in comparison to the previous years using grain-based feeds. ADM also produces excellent forage-based "treats" as well, eliminating the guilt which is sometimes associated with treating!

"No Colic, Lower Feed Cost, Simpler Routine
My Common Sense Using Good Ole Horse Sense Makes Sense To Me!
Forage-Based Feed Products—Yea!"

6. *Barefoot or Horse Shoes*:

Prior to my adult experience with horse-keeping I had never heard of horses being barefoot. Cowboy had shoes on his front feet only when I initially brought him to our farm—a common practice in our area—and for a couple of years, I routinely engaged a local farrier's services to properly maintain his shoes accordingly. It was during a natural horsemanship clinic that I attended with my Sunday Girl that someone approached me and inquired as to whether

I had ever considered leaving her barefooted. And that was my initial introduction to "barefoot trims" and to my current hoof expert and good friend, Audrey Salisbury, who works full-time operating her hoof trimming business known as Barefoot'n It.

For an excess of ten years now, I have chosen to keep all my horses barefoot, and Audrey is my go-to consultant for all things regarding hoof care and upkeep. She visits my farm every six to eight weeks for an overnight visit while she trims hooves, spends some "friendship time" and talks—a lot. In fact, we both talk a lot about everything equine related, as well as about religion, world politics, and day-to-day issues. And in spite of all that, we are still friends. Therefore, when considering the information I wished to include regarding hoof trimming and shoeing, I asked her to explain in her own words, as a hoof specialist, what she believed to be important in that regard, and this is her response:

"Over the years it has become customary for new horse owners to be told/taught that their horse must have shoes in order to be ridden. If we turn back time to the 1970s, however, our 4-H Horse and Pony Clubs taught us that it was natural for the horse to be barefoot. We were taught it was overall much healthier for the horse as well, allowing more blood flow with each stride the horse takes. Poorly-fitted shoes can restrict up to 70 percent of the blood flow. Barefooted horses are more sure-footed and do not tire as quickly. Today's progressive horse enthusiasts recognize that their previously-shoed horses benefit from being barefoot. It is important for barefooted horses to be regularly exposed to various terrain, thereby enabling the bare hoof to harden and grow properly. The horse owner must be creative in how they add gravel to heavily traveled areas in their pastures and paddocks, and recognize the need to create muddy areas as well as areas for stepping up and down. It is helpful to arrange gates from one pasture/paddock to the next in an off-set fashion, requiring horses to travel further for hay and water. Exercise, particularly walking, is invaluable.

A good source of minerals is a must for strong hooves. Low sugar and starch diets contribute to strong hooves as well.

Any horse can go barefoot. Due to their living conditions, some may have a longer period of transition than others. Gaited horses transition the quickest, many in as little as three six-week trim cycles. The average transition period is approximately four to six months. It is always best to come out of shoes as winter approaches, when the ground is still soft and muddy, allowing the horse to develop a good feel on soft ground. By spring, they are moving out totally barefoot on the trails. If no rock is introduced to their normal daily living routine, then it may be wise to use hoof boots when riding over more rugged terrain. There are also hoof coatings which can be applied to the sole of the hooves; this toughens the bottom of their hooves so they do not have to wear boots.

The average horse is not ridden enough to need shoes. The retired horse and those in rehabilitation from injuries or illness do not need shoes. Going barefoot will actually help their blood circulation and promote faster healing. Horses that suffer from hoof problems which have been caused by rigid bracing which redirects the normal hoof growth into an unnatural form, can be corrected in time with a proper barefoot trim.

The time frame between barefoot trims will vary according to the amount of exercise a horse receives, as well as the terrain on which it lives, the time of year, and how long the horse has been barefooted.

Horses that have been barefooted for three to four years or longer can easily go six to eight weeks between trims during summer; once their hooves are balanced, they begin to travel and wear them naturally. For others, five weeks is sufficient during summer and eight weeks at winter's peak when daylight hours are minimal."

From a personal standpoint, I have found barefoot to be preferable because it is simpler to maintain. I never have to worry about a loose shoe and emergency farrier visits. Nor do I have to concern myself with split hooves and nail holes. I have also noticed that in recent years a number of highly regarded race tracks no longer require shoes. The practice of shoeing was initiated *by the human* primarily for horses to be used over a variety of terrains under the care of riders who were not familiar with routine hoof trimming and care over extended periods of time. Shoes provided protection to hooves as well during an environment of war. It is mandatory, however, to engage an experienced and reputable barefoot trim expert if you decide to allow your horses to go barefoot. The actual barefoot trim is different from a farrier's trim—and it's not as easy as it may first appear!

You've Found the Horse of Your Dreams

Now that you've found the horse of your dreams—or so you think—there are still a few considerations prior to making that final commitment. Regardless of how conscientious you have been to this point, it is likely that your heart has been engaged in this process and once that happens, an unbiased and educated viewpoint may be necessary to insure that your decision is a wise one. Therefore, I have listed below a few points on which to reflect.

1. *Get a consultation from a reputable trainer.*

    Although you have found what you believe to be your UBHL and recognize that you need to be disciplined with regard to your budget, the prepurchase consultation fee charged by a reputable trainer regarding this particular horse is invaluable. Depending upon the geographic area in which you live, the fee will vary from $100 to $300 upward. The consult should involve a hands-on session between the trainer and horse, as well as an understanding by the trainer regarding your personal horsemanship goals and experience.

    Whenever I am asked to assist with this service my consultation and evaluation of the horse include the following:

    a. An interview with the potential buyer in order to evaluate their personal equine experience as well as their own perception regarding their personal skill level, horsemanship discipline interests, and overall equine goals.

b. A hands-on session with the horse in question during which I evaluate overall body condition; this includes the horse's physical as well as mental soundness. I check the horse's hooves, teeth, and rub my hands over the entire body. This includes "picking" or cleaning the hooves. By touching the horse's body, I can assess how reactive the horse tends to be, as well as potentially discover any tumors or areas of concern that should be evaluated by a vet. It is important to know prepurchase whether the horse has good ground manners, as well as determine if the horse reflects the proper respect for its handler.

c. Round pen or on-line work with the horse is necessary in order to determine the horse's response to cues as well as observe its attitude when these requests are made. Most horses fall into either a "whoa" or a "go" category; the experience of the potential owner should be considered in combination with the horse's tendencies in this area.

d. View under saddle and with full tack. Although I don't personally feel it necessary for me to ride the horse in question, I always request to see the horse under saddle. It is much simpler for me to perceive both soundness issues as well as the equine's attitude toward direction while watching someone else ride. In addition, I can request the rider to perform various transitions as necessary.

e. View trailering manners. I always have the horse "trailer load" and ideally have the horse back off as well as step forward from the trailer, depending upon the available trailer type. It is recommended that the horse always be able to back off and step down, as some trailer styles do not allow the horse turnaround room in order to walk forward out of the trailer.

f. Evaluate deworming reaction. I carry an empty dewormer paste tube with me in order to evaluate how well the horse will accept deworming. If the seller has a dewormer on hand and it is the appropriate time to administer it, I offer to do so. Although resistance to deworming is common and can be easily overcome, it is always important for the new owner to be aware of the horse's reaction, especially if the potential buyer is a novice. Administering dewormer to a resistant horse can be overwhelming to a new horse handler.

g. Observe the potential buyer with the horse. It is helpful to have the buyer watch me as I perform the above-described activities, after which I ask the buyer to work with the horse in a similar fashion. This not only allows me to evaluate the horse interacting with its new potential owner, but also enables the buyer to determine their own confidence level and ask any questions which may arise during this process.

2. *Now it's time to take a ride.*

At this point in time, the trainer has worked with the horse in question, the horse has had time to acclimate to the various handlers, and has been tacked up and ridden for evaluation purposes. Now it's your turn. Put on your helmet (yes, I said, "Put on your helmet!") and climb aboard! If you haven't already done so, this will be a moment you will log into your mental library as one of the most exciting moments of your "horse" life. Once you are in the saddle, don't be afraid to ask questions, and don't allow your "jitters" to prohibit your fun! You're not expected to be an expert rider (unless, of course, you are!) and it will take several rides for you to become comfortable with a particular horse. As I have previously mentioned, each horse has a different feel, and it may require more than one or two sessions for you to develop the proper "seat." In addition, it is unlikely that you will be using your own saddle for this particular ride, which also makes a tremendous difference in your overall riding experience.

3. *Try out a few horses you like.*

It is normal for you to be inclined to purchase this particular horse, especially if you have already invested a substantial amount of time and effort into this project. However, this may quite likely not be the perfect horse for you. Even if everything appears to be pointing in that direction, it is still important for you to ride a few other horses prior to purchasing this one. By doing so, you will either receive in your mind and heart a confirmation that this is definitely the best choice for you, or you may actually find another horse you prefer. It happens. That's why it is so important to take a step back and evaluate everything you have learned about this horse and yourself.

4. *Listen to your intuition and your trainer.*

Once you have ridden several horses and had your trainer provide their evaluation of the horse or horses in question, you will experience an intuitive or gut reaction which will likely be the direction you should seek. If you are not comfortable with a particular horse or in any way feel that horse to be dangerous or disrespectful, you should share those thoughts with your consultant/trainer and listen to their response with an open mind. You should always expect an unbiased and candid evaluation regarding the horse in question and the trainer's advice as to whether this particular horse is recommended for you.

Don't buy the wrong horse for the right person.

In the horse market, as I have previously stressed, it is *always* a "buyer's market." My personal advice is to take a step away, sleep on it, and pray about the decision. In my experience, God *always* knows best.

5. *Know your budget, and stick to it.*

As in every situation, there may be exceptions to the rule, but the amount of money you are about to invest into this purchase will likely be substantial. The initial purchase, however, is minimal in comparison to the ongoing expense for upkeep. Therefore, your ability to refrain from stepping outside of your intended purchase price will enable you to be prepared for future purchases and unexpected expenses of which there will be many.

6. *Negotiate. It's a buyer's market.*

Although I may appear to be repetitive, I would like to stress, "There is always negotiating room when purchasing a horse." Most sellers have taken the anticipation of negotiation into consideration with their initial asking price. If the prospect of negotiation is problematic for you, then ask your trainer/consultant to negotiate on your behalf. The worst scenario is that the seller refuses to sell for less than the asking price. Nothing gained, but nothing lost.

Bringing Your New Baby Home

Yea! Praise the Lord! Hallelujah! You have done your homework, found the horse of your dreams, taken care of boarding or housing arrangements, and are now ready to bring your new "baby" home. How exciting! Now you are facing another first of many challenges to come:

Transportation, Insurance, Coggins

It is unlikely that you will own a horse trailer at this point, but quite likely that the previous owner will be happy to arrange transportation for you. In fact, this is something that should be addressed during purchase negotiations. Otherwise, they or your consultant/trainer should be able to assist you in locating a reputable transporter. Be sure to address the costs involved prior to arranging transportation.

In addition, the question of insurance should be addressed; it is important for you to determine whether the transporter is properly insured, and whether that insurance includes liability as well as comprehensive coverage should your horse be injured during transport.

Current Coggins

Coggins. What in the world are *Coggins*? State law mandates that all equine be tested annually for a type of equine leukemia which is highly contagious, and can easily be transmitted during transport. This requires a blood sample, with the results taking a couple of weeks, at which time your vet will provide you with a labwork verification called a *Coggins* report. You are required to keep this report on site with the horse and within your vehicle during any and all transports.

In addition, you will be asked to provide your negative Coggins report whenever you take your horse to a new barn or to trail rides, shows, etc. I would recommend you make several copies, although a copy is not sufficient for the state highway patrol; the original must be presented for verification of negative Coggins should you be stopped during transport. In the absence of negative Coggins proof, your horse will not be allowed entry to any horse event. Failure to present same during transport will result in potential fines, and you are actually risking your horse being detained for quarantine and branding.

Each state varies regarding other documentation which may be required in order to confirm that your horse has been adequately vaccinated, and some states may require additional medical verification regarding the horse's health. It is your responsibility to verify the documents that will be required when transporting your horse across individual state lines.

Although not mandatory, I recommend that you be present if possible during the horse's loading (if within a reasonable distance) and most definitely present at the point of delivery.

This will enable you to confirm that all proper travel documentation is current and available for inspection. Your presence at the time of loading will also allow you to examine your horse's condition prior to travel; minor cuts, scratches, and abrasions which are noted prior to travel will not be a source of conflict between you and the transporter when the horse reaches its destination.

Section 4

Working with Your

Horse:

The Practical Side

The Gentle Spirit REWARD Technique

Your new *horse baby* has finally arrived, and both you and the horse have managed to survive without permanent injury or death!

What to Do Next?

With the presumption having been made that your housing, feed, stable supplies, and pasture needs have all been adequately met, my very first word of advice is an adamant "Don't ride yet!" Tacking up your horse and jumping on to ride before allowing him/her to settle in to the new environment is tantamount to giving a sixteen-year-old boy keys to a new sports car before he has ever driven a motor vehicle. The potential for an accident is monumental. In fact, both you and the horse need some relationship-building time. A few days to bond with each other through grooming and ground work will do wonders toward confidence building and trust between human and horse.

Horses are animals of prey, and they will initially view everything around them in their new environment as a potential predator; that includes humans. They are hardwired to think accordingly; this primary instinct has enabled them to survive in the wild for thousands of years. Domesticated horses must be *taught* to trust humans in order to maintain a calm and stable mindset. A thorough recognition of this predator-prey relationship is necessary by you in order to safely ride and interact with your horse on a daily basis.

Most people have been told that "a horse will sense your fear of him and will in turn take advantage of that as a weakness." In fact, the exact opposite is true: A horse does indeed sense your energy of fear, tension, or anxiety. But then, it interprets this fearful energy with a thought process that is saying, "I sense fear and nervousness. I must be in danger. I don't know what the danger is, but I need to get away from it—now!" That is the premise that causes a horse to rear, buck, run, or otherwise "act the fool." The horse in most situations is simply trying to remove itself from what it considers a threat to its survival.

By the same token, horses sense calm, balanced energy as well. A horse handler exuding a calm, confident sense of purpose will enable the horse to relax and "listen" for their direction and leadership. Horses respond in a positive manner to leadership and a firm yet gentle sense of discipline. Much like children, they *prefer*, rather than resent, strong sensitive leaders. Like canines, they live in the moment, and in most cases strive to please the leaders they trust.

With these things in mind, the ongoing training of both human and horse will progress and change on a daily, sometimes moment-to-moment, basis. Regarding the type of training approach to be used by you and your horse, it should be noted that there are multiple training techniques and recognized trainers by the dozens. I recommend that you seek out the method of training which best suits your personality and skill level. Similar to the manner you used in seeking out the horse of your choice, you will need to research training videos, books, various clinicians (both local and via Internet or television), and local equine events in order to determine a learning and training method with which you are comfortable.

Equine skills and horsemanship are perpetual; you will soon discover that the more you learn, the more you need and want to learn. Because both the human and the horse are living beings who grow and change daily, our training and level of understanding changes likewise. I, personally, am a *seeker*. I am constantly seeking to be a better person, and therefore a better "horse person" as well. After and through my learning experiences with various clinicians' methods, I managed to glean a basic understanding of horsemanship, merging certain facets from each in order to become comfortable with my own personal training approach, which I refer to as the "Gentle Spirit REWARD Technique". The name of my farm is Gentle Spirit Stables, and I named it as such in honor of and in tribute to the Holy Spirit. I regard the Holy Spirit as a Great but Gentle Spirit, and I envision the Holy Spirit as a soft gentle breath which encompasses and wraps me in safety. By that same token, I have selected the horses here on my farm based upon them each having a sweet, gentle spirit and a softness that is strong yet pliable. Therefore, it is only natural that I chose to use a strong yet gentle training method in order to produce and focus on the best and most positive traits in my horses as well as myself and those around me.

The Gentle Spirit REWARD Technique is simple and will lend itself toward any type of horse discipline as well as provide a simple "cure" for most horse issues and problems:

> R – Request an action.
> E – Expect the right answer.
> W – Wait (as long as it takes) for proper response.
> A – Accept the slightest try.
> R – Reward with release the correct response.
> D – Do it all again!

To further elaborate on the REWARD Technique:

Request an action: This can be any type of request, using cues which are easily recognized and understood by both human and horse. For example, you can ask the horse to lower its head by pressing your hand on the top of horse's poll. You should press downward with the tips of your fingers using a verbal cue if desired, such as "Down."

Expect the right answer: Maintain this pressure while expecting the horse's head to lower.

Wait for proper response: Do not release this pressure for as long as it takes for the horse to respond.

Accept the slightest try: The instant you feel the horse's head lower even the slightest bit, release the pressure! This seemingly insignificant response to your hand pressure is considered a "try."

Reward with release the correct response: Horses learn from the release—not from the pressure. Therefore your instant release of pressure at the point of their slightest try will communicate to them that you are requesting them to drop their head.

Do it all again: As soon as you get your first try and have released the pressure, wait a few moments. Then do it again! As you wait a few moments between tries, watch your horse for signs that he/she is absorbing the lesson. This may be reflected in a number of ways such as licking and chewing or a long sigh.

Although it will be necessary to repeat these lessons until the horse is performing the task at the level you are requesting, it is important that you are sensitive to the horse's ability to focus and their willing attitude. Lengthy lessons tend to backfire in balkiness; however, short lessons with a variety of tasks will produce a better response.

If you are alert to the horse's attention span by being aware of his/her body language, fewer repetitions are necessary. In order to learn the horse's natural body language and to engage in better communication, which is a two-way conversation with your horse, I cannot overly stress the importance of *eye contact*.

Therefore, do not—I repeat—do not wear opaque sunglasses!

If the horse cannot see your eyes, you cannot expect a willingness to communicate with you. Between you and your horse, the eyes are indeed the windows to the soul.

Although many clinicians and various trainers make reference to having the horse give you "two eyes," I have never heard anyone address the fact that the horse should be able to see our eyes as well. I do know that horses use their eyes to communicate with one another; a direct seemingly insignificant "look" from an alpha horse will get a quick response from the horse to whom it is directed. If that initial look is ignored, it is quickly followed by a head movement or "ear pinning." The look, however, is their first outward form of communication. Therefore, our human effort to use natural horsemanship techniques to communicate with our horses requires us to use a language they can easily comprehend by engaging our own eyes as our first point of communication. An easier point of reference is to imagine the stern look a mother gives a misbehaving child as her first warning to redirect that child's behavior. The pressure provided through eye contact is readily recognized by your horse, similar to their ability to sense our energy, whether calm and reassuring or anxious and fearful.

As your personal progress continues in regard to training techniques and horsemanship skills, you will develop a progressive understanding of how your body cues and subtle movements are perceived by the horse. This will be particularly relevant if you choose to develop a personal relationship with a particular horse and are willing to learn that horse's individual sensibilities. Horses as living creatures are affected by their genetic predisposition as well as their environment, and are therefore to some degree different from one to another. The time we spend observing and interacting with our horses will heighten our own awareness and understanding as to the best training approach for each.

The Basics

In addition to having obtained a fundamental understanding of your horsemanship goals, there are a few basic skill sets at which you should be proficient prior to or at the very least immediately after bringing your new horse home. I know this from my own personal experience, as I can readily recall a number of my own inadequacies shortly after Cowboy's arrival here at the farm. I later learned that my shortcomings were common issues for new horse owners and could be easily addressed:

Lifting and cleaning the horse's hooves is one of the most common fear-invoking challenges for new horse owners. The possibility of being kicked is quite real, and the proper method and regular practice of lifting the horse's leg is essential for good horse husbandry. Most horses that have been properly trained are easily cued to lift their legs for you, allowing you to safely clean their hooves as often as required. You should not hesitate to ask your trainer to assist you in learning the best technique for this. The horse is able to support its entire body weight on its other legs while lifting its hoof for you; you should not allow the horse to place their weight on you, nor lean on you for support. In addition, if your body placement is proper you will be able to anticipate and actually feel the musculature of the horse's shoulder prior to any potential attempt to kick or otherwise pull away from your grasp. As with all other training issues, do not allow the horse to withdraw its hoof from you until you have completed your task. A smart horse will occasionally test your ability in this area; be cognizant of this, and position yourself in a manner which will enable you to maintain a firm grasp on the hoof until you allow the horse freedom to place it on the ground. Should he/she pull the hoof away prior to your completion of the task, you should immediately repeat the lifting of the leg, establishing to the horse that you are in control, thereby preventing this from recurring in the future.

"Catching" and haltering your horse shouldn't be problematic if you have already established a connection with your horse, and presuming you have applied at least a few of the common sense techniques recommended in earlier chapters of this book, the "catching" and haltering of your horse will not be an issue. However, once your horse is pastured, you may find that he/she is not always eager to be haltered, especially once the horse realizes that haltering may mean he/she is expected to work. Most horses when given the option to either eat and graze or work will choose to eat. Enticing the horse to approach you through the use of food treats is essentially not harmful, but over the course of time, your goal should be to have the horse come to you with or without the lure of treats. You should always approach your horse for haltering with a particular plan in your mind, as with all training exercises. Your halter should be previously made ready for placement with the lead rope available to lay across the horse's neck as soon as the approach is achieved and the horse is within easy reach. This should be accomplished in a calm, smooth, and easy motion. Once the lead rope is over your horse's neck, the treat can be presented (if appropriate) during which time the process of having the horse place his/her head into the halter can be implemented. There is no substitute for practice in learning this simple, yet somewhat challenging task. If you are unsure of yourself, ask your trainer or other experienced equine enthusiast to demonstrate this process for you.

Also be aware of your body language while approaching your horse; direct your focus beside the horse's body rather than toward the head. A head-on direct approach will be perceived by the horse as a signal to turn and move away from you; remember the concept of "eye pressure." Pressure, either with your body or with a riding stick, which is directed in front of the horse's withers, will signal the horse to turn away; pressure directed behind the front shoulder, in contrast, is perceived as a driving pressure and indicates to the horse a direction to move forward. Therefore, your horse is more likely to stand and wait for you as you approach if you walk in a parallel fashion toward his/her body. Technically, you are not directing pressure toward your horse with either your eyes or your body. Once you are standing directly beside your horse's head and neck, you are in a proper position to gently lay the lead rope across its neck. I find that a soft touch to the side of my horse's face and neck prior to placement of the lead rope is reassuring to the horse, and generally does not prompt the horse to move away from me. In this fashion, you are not actually catching the horse, but rather having him/her "join up" with you as the leader. This is highly preferable to the cat and mouse game frequently seen as some folks attempt to halter their horse; this game is never actually won by the human, with their final effort being that of returning to the barn for a feed bucket, which ultimately lures the horse for haltering. Again, practice makes perfect; always have a plan and be prepared before entering your horse's pasture.

In reference to the type of halter to be used, I have learned through experience and clinicians' advice to use a knotted rope halter for all training and exercise routines rather than a flat web halter. The knotted rope halter—especially when used with a twelve- to fourteen-foot lead rope—allows me to easily control and provide direction to the horse. The knots are designed for placement in areas on the horse's jaw and face at particularly sensitive pressure points, whereby the slightest movement of the lead rope can be felt by the horse. A flat web halter broadens out the pressure we attempt to apply and does not provide the horse with the ability to feel the movement of the rope. With a flat web halter, we find ourselves in a tug of war between us and the horse. Who do you think is likely to win?

A flat web halter is necessary for use whenever the horse is being trailered or otherwise tied for a period of time, as the knotted rope halter, if used for tying purposes, will create an insensitivity in the areas of the knots, as well as abrasions. It should be noted that a knotted rope halter should *never* be worn underneath the bridle.

Tacking up your horse, especially for the first time, can be a daunting challenge unless you have previously practiced this process with the assistance of your trainer. The proper fit and placement of your saddle and bridle is mandatory for your safety. By this point in time, you should have engaged your trainer to assist you by using the same equipment which you will be using once the horse is home. The correct bit and proper saddle fit as well as an understanding of the tightness and security of the cinch is essential. Most trainers suggest that the cinch be checked for tightness three different times: when the saddle is initially secured; after the horse has moved its feet a bit—perhaps lunged; and prior to mounting. If you detect that the saddle is loose at any point in time, whether during the mounting process or while riding, always retighten the cinch to your satisfaction. It should be noted, however, that overly tightened saddles do not allow the horse to breathe and move freely, and can result in poor behavior by the horse. There is a happy medium at which point the saddle is adequately secure and the horse is comfortable; you will become familiar and comfortable in this knowledge over a period of time.

One of the most important recommendations I believe to be pertinent in regard to the cinching process is that the cinch be tightened gradually, smoothly, and gently, rather than using a harsh heavy tug as we often see. The harsh quick tightening of the cinch is uncomfortable to the horse and can ultimately cause the horse to become "cinchy." It also creates a sense of distrust by the horse for the handler. Many horses who have been handled in this manner will actually try to bite the handler and at the very least try to move away from the cinching process.

Be willing to take a few riding lessons. Don't let pride—nor your pocketbook—prevent you from taking a few lessons from a reputable trainer once you have your horse at home. You have accomplished your dream of locating the best horse for you and have likely invested a substantial amount of cash toward this goal; do not stop just short of success by failing to engage assistance to help you with the knowledge and training necessary.

If you are insecure in any area as it pertains to your horse, you will find yourself unwilling to ride and otherwise interact with your new UBHL. No question will be perceived as silly by an understanding and proficient instructor. Your brain will likely be filled with questions, but your trainer/instructor cannot read your mind. Be candid with them and do not hesitate to acknowledge any areas of fear or anxiety. In all likelihood, they have experienced similar feelings in the past. Their goal should be to provide you with the knowledge you need to gain a confident seat and full enjoyment of your horse.

The wise do not hesitate to seek wisdom.

Common Sense Tips and Tidbits Make Your Horse Life Happier and Simpler!

As in any project, whether recreational or work-related, there are generally a number of acceptable methods to accomplish one's goal. My daddy always told me, however, that I should seek the best *and* simplest way for myself. Therefore, I am presenting a number of common sense tips which I have learned over the years as they pertain to some of the most common horse-related issues. Use your own common sense in the application of any advice provided according to your personal equine needs, and always confer with your veterinarian regarding the specific needs of your horse.

Preventing Colic

1. Never make sudden changes to your horse's feeding routine. All feed changes should be made gradually by integrating the new hay or feed over the course of a three- to seven-day time frame.
2. Spring grasses contain more sugar in the initial growth period. Whenever turning your horse out to graze on new grass, limit initial grazing time to thirty minutes, gradually increasing over a period of days. After several days, your horse should be able to graze at will without colic issues.

3. Sudden weather changes can cause some horses to colic, especially when experiencing a sudden drop in temperature; that is, cold, wet weather following a period of warm balmy temperatures. If your horse tends to colic with extreme weather changes some preventive common sense measures may assist you in warding off this type of "weather-colic." Keep an eye on your local weather forecasts; a day or two before the inclement weather arrives, there are a number of dietary changes that can be considered, depending on the individual horse's tendency toward colic. Some of these may include a bran mash, added salt to increase water intake, or corn oil administered with their feed; you should consult your equine veterinarian or nutritionist regarding their recommendation as it pertains to your particular horse's needs.

4. Always provide clean, temperate water around the clock. In cold winter months, a heated bucket will prevent water temperatures from dipping below about fifty-five degrees. If you do not have access to electricity, fill a two-liter plastic bottle with water to approximately half-full and place in the drinking bucket. The movement of the floating bottle will help prevent freezing. Always check the water each morning, making sure to remove ice blocks. During hot summer months, water should be kept in a cool area out of direct sunlight. Most horses drink between eleven to fifteen gallons of water daily.

5. If you notice your horse is not drinking enough, sprinkle a tablespoon of salt over their feed. Keeping a salt/mineral block available should also increase their thirst.

6. Never give new foods and human food without checking reliable sources regarding horse toxicity.

7. Keep a check on any potential weeds, shrubs, and trees in and surrounding your pasture. Many common shrubs and weeds are toxic to horses.

8. Bring water from home for your horse to drink while trailering. See item 3 under "Traveling and Trailering."

9. Ingestion by your horse of sand and dirt over a period of time can cause "sand colic." You should be aware of hay placement as well as grazing conditions as they pertain to sand. Horses tend to lick their lips frequently while eating, and if allowed to graze in sandy areas will ingest excessive dirt. This sand and dirt may not pass through the intestinal tract, settling in the horse's gut, and ultimately result in an episode of colic. Diarrhea is sometimes an early indicator of sand in the intestinal canal. Your due diligence in providing areas for eating which prevent ingesting of sand can prevent this occurrence. There are methods which can be used to determine whether your horse is likely to have sand colic; there are a number of remedies for this type of colic as well, and they should be discussed with your veterinarian.

Traveling and Trailering

1. Always back your horse off a trailer. Although it's more nerve-racking at first than walking off in a forward manner, your horse will not develop the *habit* of being able to walk forward. Remember, you can't turn a horse around in a slant load or side-by-side trailer. You never want to bring a new horse home and realize after a four-hour drive that the horse will not back off your new slant load trailer! Been there, done that, and it didn't take but once to learn that lesson!

2. Before buying a new horse and/or bringing your horse home, ask the owner as to the horse's ability to load and unload. Always have this demonstrated *before* the purchase.

3. When hauling your horse to a new location, bring water from home whenever possible. All water sources taste different, and your horse will be hesitant to drink

water with a different smell or taste. For long trips, your vet may recommend use of an electrolyte; there are a variety of brands available through most equine catalog supply sources.

4. Regularly check the temperature in your trailer when hauling. Make sure your horse is neither sweating nor too chilled. A light blanket may be necessary if hauling in chilly night air. Make sure there is adequate ventilation but that the horse is not in direct wind flow while driving, and *never* allow the horse's head to remain outside a window during travel!

5. Routinely allow your horse to trailer load, especially when there are long periods of time between trips. This is similar to dancing; a little practice all along keeps it fresh in your mind. Otherwise, your horse will pick the next important loading time to resist going onboard, and I can guarantee it will be when you are on a tight schedule!

6. Check your spare trailer tire to make sure it's the right size and type! Invest in a tire lift that enables you to change the tire without unloading your horse. Also check your travel insurance carrier to find out whether they will change a flat for you without unloading. The thought of unloading your horse and standing along the side of a busy interstate is traumatizing.

7. Check your tire pressure before each trip. Purchase new tires every seven years (minimum) regardless of miles used. Tires dry rot over time.

8. Never open the side "man door" and walk away from your horse. Horses will be tempted to exit through the opening, regardless of the fact that their body will not fit. Many horses have been stuck in the side man door! In fact, I personally know of a horse that tried to exit a custom-designed window by stepping onto a feeding bench in the trailer; the poor horse was found hanging half in and half

out by the terrified owner and was ultimately rescued by an ingenuous farmer and horror-struck owner.

9. If possible, unlatch the tail bar (on side-by-side trailers) prior to opening the door. The horse is subject to step back as soon as the door is opened, and if he/she steps back while the tail bar is still latched, the horse will be trapped between trailer bed and tail bar, possibly resulting in a serious leg injury.

10. Do not feed grain while trailering. A small amount of hay can be fed if the trip is over a several hour period. Short trips (an hour or less) will not require any hay.

11. Bring hay and feed from home adequate to last the length of a round trip.

12. Make sure you have purchased truck tags that allow you to haul an adequate amount of weight per your state's regulations.

13. Use a flat web halter while hauling. Knotted rope halters will cause pressure rubs due to the movement of the trailer. This can result in physical as well as training issues.

14. Keep a check on your floors beneath your trailer mats. Wood floors rot! Keep them dry and clean.

15. Check your signal and brake lights before every trip.

16. *Never* throw out burning cigarette butts. An otherwise harmless cigarette butt has been known to bounce/fly into a horse trailer loaded with horses and hay, causing a huge catastrophic fire.

17. Apply a small amount of common vapor rub on horse's nose, especially when traveling or trail-riding to help prevent your horse, whether male or female, from scenting a mare in season or other scents that may be unsettling to your horse. Do it a few times during your normal routine—prior to travel—to accustom your horse to the vapor rub odor.

Grooming

1. Horses do not need routine water baths! If you enjoy bathing and pampering your horse that's great, but recognize that you're doing it to satisfy your own needs rather than those of your horse. It does, however, provide relationship-building time. Horses prefer to take a good roll in freshly cut grass or clean sand as opposed to a water bath (which, by the way, they will immediately do as soon as you finish their water bath and allow them access to an open area). If you are grooming them just prior to taking them to a show or other event that mandates that they be clean, you should cover them with an appropriate horse sheet as soon as your grooming is complete and they are dry.

2. Regular brushing with proper equine brushes and tools will allow the horse's natural body oils to do their job. The horse's hair, when properly brushed, will help maintain their body temperature as well as prevent sunburn.

3. Picking or cleaning the hooves as often as possible (preferably at least once daily) is required, not optional. Horses pick up pebbles, nails, and other hard debris which can debilitate a horse unless removed before permanent damage to the sole or hoof wall occurs. Hoof cleaning is one of the most frequent fears among new horse owners. Please review the previous chapter to familiarize yourself and become comfortable with this challenge.

4. Some horses are more sensitive or "tender-skinned" than others. When grooming, always brush hair in the direction in which it grows. As one would work out a tangle in our own hair, be gentle and always work the tail and mane hair from the ends upward to prevent pulling and unnecessary loss of hair. Hair takes an excess of an entire year to grow from the tail head to the ground. If

you want a long, luxurious tail, you should remove tangles and knots as soon as they develop to prevent breakage. Note: The grooming process should be enjoyable to both you and your horse. If your horse shows signs of agitation (such as foot stomping or constant moving away from you) then you are likely causing discomfort. Determine the problem and make a correction; however, do *not* stop the grooming process until your horse is calm and relaxed. As with any training lesson, to cease an activity while your horse is expressing resistance will teach him that his bad behavior will allow him to have his way.

I have found that the use of firm, assertive language is necessary on occasion to remind my UBHL, Sunday, to correct her attitude. She has never been particularly fond of grooming (and is quite tender-skinned); her nature is to stomp a front foot when she is not in the mood for grooming. After first reminding myself to be gentler with her, I then promptly remind her to be patient with a firm assertive "No!" or "Stop!" This works every time with her because we have developed a close relationship. Patience is the key.

It is important for me to point out, however, that until one has built this relationship it is prudent to recognize that the stomp is in fact a warning from your horse that they have had enough. It can in some cases be the precursor to a bite or a kick; I experienced this firsthand with my Shetland pony after two hours of picking sand spurs from her long fetlock hair and tail. Her multiple unheeded warnings to me were followed by a swift "cow kick" planted directly on my mouth as I knelt beside her. In retrospect, I should have given her a break, stopping at a point in time when she was not being disrespectful to me. For additional indicators of warnings, see the segment below regarding this.

5. There are thousands upon thousands of grooming products, made for every conceivable notion. Most of them aren't necessary to the average horse owner. Save some of your grooming budget, and be more selective with your purchases. Most human hair products work well on horses, with the exception of those containing tea tree ingredients. I have made a habit of bringing home complimentary motel hair products which I dilute approximately 50/50 with water. These work great, and I particularly like shampoo/conditioner mixtures. It is mandatory, however, that the product be diluted; otherwise, the amount of suds will be overwhelming and impossible to completely rinse. I also keep an eye out for shampoo product sales, using common sense regarding the type of shampoo. Keep in mind that your horse has coarse, tangle-prone hair. Also, I do not recommend using any specialty shampoos intended for humans such as dandruff shampoos, etc.

I also keep on hand at all times an iodine solution shampoo which is intended for equines and should be used on occasion for manure soiled hair as well as for the prevention of "rain-rot" and other fungal or bacterial needs.

The most impressive product I have ever used for detangling is Cowboy Magic Detangler; it is miraculous in the removal of knots and tangles. Some horses are genetically predisposed to curly manes which create a nightmare of tangles and braids. Cowboy Magic is the only product I have found that not only aids in the removal of these dreaded knots, but also helps in the prevention of tangling as well. Hats off to the folks who produce that product; it is worth every cent. It took me eleven years of trial and error with other products before I tried it, but from this point forward, Cowboy Magic is the only detangling product I will endorse.

6. When grooming, never ever—did I say never?—apply detangling or sheen-inducing products on the saddle or

girth areas. Picture the application of silicon to the bottom of your shoes and then walking across an icy floor. *Slippery* is not what you want your saddle to be! Avoid spraying or wiping any such product onto that area of your horse. Period. This includes oil-based pest control sprays as well.

7. Hot water or cold water, that is the question. Whether it is necessary to use warm water as opposed to cold water when bathing and rinsing your horse—different folks, different strokes! Some professionals have no objection to cold water regardless of cool temperatures. However, I personally will not use frigidly cold water on cold days. If I find it necessary to rinse or bathe my horse, I do everything possible to use moderately warm water. I have found that my horses react much more favorably if the water is temperate.

In addition, many people are advised to spray their horses with cold water on exceedingly hot days or after a sweaty hot ride in order to cool them down. Some of us old-timers think it best *not* to spray cold water on very hot days, as we have seen several cases of pneumonia resulting from this routine. Better to use a sweat scraper and provide shade and fans than to spray with cold water. Wiping down the extremely hot horse with a cool wet towel is preferable to the cold water spray. Common sense, folks, common sense! And your horse will thank you. Think of it this way: A horse's skin is so sensitive that it easily feels a fly pitch on it; imagine how cold water must feel. Consider temperate rather than cold water if you feel you must absolutely spray your horse.

Bugs and Pests

1. Stable flies, house flies, horse flies, deer flies, and gnats, gnats, gnats!

   Our farm is in the southeastern United States and we have all of the above and more. I just recently realized that flies and gnats are named as one of the plagues of the apocalypse. I am praying not to be present at that time! But for the present time, I do find myself always on the lookout for the easiest as well as the most efficient and cost effective way to keep these nasty pests at by.

   We house ten to twelve horses here at any given time, making fly prevention of utmost importance. Obviously, manure removal and control is necessary. However, the best fly control has proven to be a combination of garlic powder as a feed supplement—I highly recommend Springtime Inc.'s brand of products—used in combination with "Fly Predators" that I order from Spalding Fly Predators. Garlic powder and Fly Predators are "green" methods of keeping flies under control without exposing myself, my family, and my horses to pesticides. Garlic powder as a feed supplement permeates the horse's body and feces, and although humans cannot normally detect a garlic odor, most flies are repelled by the scent. I have used and highly recommend a variety of Springtime Inc. products, including their joint supplements for horses as well as dogs. Although your horse (or dog) may initially resist the garlic taste/smell, they quickly become familiar with its scent and taste if given routinely.

   Fly Predators consume fly larvae before the flies hatch, and the use of these tiny insects have proven year after year to be phenomenal. Small shipments of unhatched Fly Predators arrive via mail during the warm months of the year, and I simply distribute them throughout the pastures and stable areas where fresh manure is most prevalent. The impact they have had on the fly population has been amazing. I only use fly and bug repellent as needed for horse flies, deer flies, and bots, particularly when I am riding or otherwise working with the horses.

Gnat control is best accomplished with fly masks for the horses when necessary. In addition, a homemade remedy of petroleum jelly in combination with a few drops of camphor oil repels them without the use of commercial products. I apply this concoction around my ears and face, and in a similar fashion on my horses. The camphor fragrance is pleasant and nontoxic.

During particularly bad infestations, I spray the fly masks with a commercial equine fly and gnat repellent before placing it on the horse. Water-based repellents are tidier and won't leave your horse with an oily residue. Note: When using fly masks be sure to remove them at nightfall and always check the areas underneath the mask for abrasions, etc.

2. Snakes and Rodents...

Snakes are drawn to areas where they can easily hide and have access to food, including birds, frogs, and rodents. Rodents are attracted to similar areas, particularly where they can locate dropped feed pellets and other edibles, including trash can areas which may contain partially eaten food items. Step back and take a look at the property where your horse is housed and pastured. Remove brush and wood piles from pastures, as well as declutter your tool, equipment, feed, and bucket areas, thereby eliminating nesting and hiding places. Be cognizant of loose feed that may be dropped, disposing of any garbage; trash receptacles with covered lids are suggested.

Refrain from the placement of bird houses and feeders near your stable and feed areas; snakes will be present wherever they detect birds.

In addition, if you live in an area that is prone to snakes, moth balls as well as sulfur can be distributed in areas to deter their entry. Commercial snake repellents are available at most hardware and garden centers as well. However, do not place these items in an area accessible to your horse's reach; some horses (and dogs) are curious and may attempt to ingest them.

Squirrels are also a nuisance, especially if they have access to feed and tack areas. During their nesting season, I have had squirrels chew a portion of the leather from a saddle, as well as destruct paper towel rolls, feed bags, and several other bedding type materials left in my open farm utility vehicle. Peppermint oil is a good squirrel deterrent; it has a pleasant scent and is nontoxic.

3. Fire Ants

Fire ants are becoming more and more of a nuisance in our particular area. You should be watchful for these ant hills in your pasture areas. Your horses should not be allowed to graze or have access to areas with fire ants; whether the horse is grazing or taking a roll in the grass, a fire ant attack on your horse can wreak havoc. If you choose to use a commercial fire ant pesticide, be aware that your horses as well as your dogs will be attracted to eat the sweet taste of the pesticide. Do not allow access until you are certain that it has completely dissolved.

Warnings from Your Horse

The horse's body language literally speaks for itself, and it is important for you to be aware of the message they are trying to convey. If you observe a group of horses, you will notice that they are continually communicating with one another. Every herd includes a leader, commonly known as the alpha, and this leader is always keeping a watchful eye on the rest of the herd, moving them from one place to another and otherwise directing them with their body energy and movement to remind them of the pecking order. Some of the more commonly recognized signals and warnings include direct eye contact, foot stomping, ear pinning, tail swishing, head and body movement, biting or nipping, and kicking. In your interaction with horses, it is essential that you are always on alert regarding any of these warnings. A tail swish and/or swift body movement is sometimes the precursor to a kick or a bite, neither of which should ever be tolerated. Although horses continually move their ears in a variety of directions to be attuned to their surroundings, a horse who displays their ears pinned tightly backward against their head is normally reflecting extreme irritability; this display should not be ignored. The cause of such should be immediately determined and remedied to avoid injury. In many cases, the human is injured as a result of a horse showing aggression toward a pasture mate; it is never a good idea to come between two horses who may be displaying rude behavior toward one another. This occurs at feeding time in particular. When entering a pasture where there are two or more horses, I make it a practice to carry a riding crop or a similar equine tool to provide myself with an area of safety surrounding my body. My swishing of this tool while walking is perceived by the horse as my tail swishing; they stay a few feet away. Swinging my arms has a similar effect, as well as doing the "chicken wing dance" with my elbows! My neighbors must get a hoot out of watching my antics, but I do whatever is necessary to stay out of harm's way—and out of the "kicking zone."

Horses are not predators and are not normally aggressive toward humans. However, they do routinely reestablish their pecking order, and as their human, I am included within this process. I make it a point to establish myself at the top of their herd each time I interact with them. This requires minimal effort, such as having them move away from me, stay out of my personal boundary space, and to wait calmly before I dump their feed into their feed tray. Although it is rewarding to have your horse nuzzle you and look for treats in your pockets, this behavior can quickly become dangerous; a pushy horse does not make for a happy human. If your horse is pushing you around, this is an indication that you have become underneath him/her in the herd pecking order, and eventually this will evolve into bad behavior under saddle.

Miscellaneous

1. Verbal Cues, Names, and Sounds

During the training of your horse, you will likely teach them at least a few verbal cues, including the sound of their name. It is important for you to keep these cues and verbal sounds simple and easy to recognize. As an example, the common word "Whoa" can sound like "No," so I choose to use the word "Stop" when I am expressing disapproval of an unacceptable behavior. My horses are also taught to recognize the word "Stand" if I want them to stand in a particular spot; if they take a step away, I use "Stand" rather than "Whoa," as it is preferable to use "Whoa" in other circumstances. "Stand" means exactly that—to stand still. In addition, it is preferable to use body cues *together* with your verbal cues in order to have them recognize each. My horses, for instance, recognize that the holding up of my index finger means to "Stand." Repetition and reward is the key to their recognition of your cues; the previous chapter explains this concept in more detail.

Another aspect of verbal sounds includes the concept that we should avoid creating a cue which mimics the sound of a predator; that is, the hissing sound made by a snake. Many people are also of the mindset that we should not name our horses using a name with negative connotations, such as Diablo or Trouble, in that the energy of our constant use of that name will sometimes evolve into a self-fulfilling prophecy.

2. Desensitize your horse to flash lights, head lights, infrared lights, camera flashes, cell phone tones, flags waving, shrill whistling, and popping or crackling sounds. Horses are hardwired to flee from any sounds or sights that may be perceived as fire or lightning.

3. Wear your riding helmet around your horse routinely in order for them to associate the helmet with you as the rider. Beware that some children wear helmets with odd shapes and décor which may appear to the horse as an unknown predator. We all look distinctly different when wearing our helmets.

4. Rain coats and hoods tend to spook most horses until they are desensitized to them. Don't wait until it's raining to expose your horse to your rain gear.

5. Wear shoes or boots with a distinct heel while riding. This will help prevent your foot from slipping through the stirrup.

6. In preparing this book segment, I inquired of my personal vet, Dr. Karen M. Bullock, as to any common-sense tip she would like to suggest. Without hesitation, she stated that the most frequent issue she encounters is in regard to whether a horse should be tied during medical examinations or procedures. Her recommendation is based upon the equine's natural instinct to flee when frightened; horses are hardwired to pull back or otherwise flee from perceived danger or predators. Therefore, when a horse is uneasy or uncomfortable with a procedure or administration of vaccinations or dewormers, the horse is less likely to harm itself or surrounding humans if it is allowed to move its feet and work through that initial instinct to pull back or

flee. Although it has become commonplace to tie a horse to a fixed object for farrier visits and medical procedures, as well as for regular grooming, this practice results in far more injuries to the human and the horse should the horse panic at any point in time while tied. Dr. Bullock always asks that the horse *not* be cross-tied or tied to fixed objects during her examinations and for most medical procedures, but rather held by a loose rein in an area which she deems safe for both human and horse.

My personal experience in this area has evolved completely during my adult horse life, from initially believing that my horses should be tied for all grooming, vetting, and hoof trimming. In fact, it has now been years since I routinely tied our horses for any purpose other than for training or while being trailered; this includes pregnancy exams, gelding procedures, teeth "floating," and all hoof work. You should always discuss this option with your personal vet, farrier, and other equine handlers who interact with you and your horse, understanding that they may not be in agreement, but recognizing that it is ultimately your decision to engage professionals whose approach to horsemanship are similar to your own.

7. Always remain alert when riding or interacting with your horse. Over a period of time, we begin to think our horses are completely predictable, and as humans we tend to think our personal horse "loves" us and would never intentionally bring us harm. Although we can, in some circumstances, develop a "relationship" with our horse, it is prudent for us to remember that horses are animals, and even the most predictable and gentle-natured horse is not 100 percent bombproof.

8. Don't humanize your horse. The human brain is designed to allow the right and left sides of our brain to interact and share information seen with each eye operating

congruently, causing us to reach logical conclusions; this same collaboration controls our reactive impulses by the application of our logic and reasoning ability. The equine brain, however, does not operate in this fashion. Each side of the horse's brain is independent of the other. In fact, this is the reasoning behind the training practice of "teaching both sides" of the horse; each eye operates independently of the other and its perception is processed on that particular side of the horse's brain. Each side of the equine brain must be trained individually, and you will most likely notice that the horse more readily accepts a particular training exercise better on or from one side as opposed to the other. Trainers commonly refer to horses using either the "reactive" side or the "thinking" side of their brain; your goal is to evoke the thinking side of your horse's brain during your riding and daily interactions, as this will be more rewarding and will bring about a safer response for both you and your horse. As with most human beings who are either left-handed or right-handed, horses tend to be more left-sided or right-sided. In general, a particular horse will prefer, as an example, to circle either to the left or to the right. In order to induce the horse into the thinking side of his/her brain, the handler or rider can direct the horse in the opposing direction; this will require the horse to "think" about the instruction, follow through as directed, and therein recognize that the handler is in control.

9. Be aware of the horse's "kicking" zones. All horses given certain circumstances are known to kick. Although unintended, many humans are injured as a result of startling a horse from behind. Although a horse's vision allows an almost panoramic 360-degree view, there is a small area in the center of its back as well as the direct center between each eye that cannot be seen by the horse.

When approaching from behind or walking around the horse, it is recommended that we should speak to the horse in a calm voice, avoiding jerky unexpected motions until the horse is aware of our presence; that is, avoid motions and movement which may be perceived by the horse as a predator on attack.

10. Although most horse enthusiasts (myself included) are gratified by feeding our equine buddies special treats by hand, most veterinarians and professional trainers recommend that treats be placed in the horse's feed bucket rather than being presented by hand. It is commonly believed that hand feeding will ultimately result in a pushy horse and eventually lead to nips and bites in an effort to seek out treats. I will admit, however, that none of my horses are known to bite or nip, and I have always fed their treats by hand. Perhaps my particular little herd recognizes that I am their "alpha mare," and as a result they haven't displayed this particular behavior with me. I felt it prudent to present the professional's recommendation *not* to feed by hand, although it is ultimately your decision. If you begin to notice pushy behavior or your horse becomes nippy, be aware that hand feeding could be the cause and should be eliminated.

11. It is normal for your horse to take short naps while standing; you may frequently notice your horse standing with head lowered and a hind foot cocked. This is usually indicative of the horse sleeping. On occasion, you will see your horse lying down with its head resting in a sort of upright position and less often with his/her head and body completely prone on the ground. These short periods of sleep usually occur only when the horse feels completely safe and secure from potential threats and predators. If you notice your horse in a prone position for more than twenty to thirty minutes, you should check on its well-being, as

lengthy periods in a reclining position are detrimental to the horse's circulation and general health. Foals as well as older horses tend to lie down for longer periods of time, but a watchful eye is recommended.

12. Dew poisoning, also known as "scratches," is a common fungal type of infection that can occur in horses who are exposed to marshy, wet, or otherwise dewy pastures or paddocks over a lengthy period of time. It is prevalent in wet spring and fall weather conditions. Should you notice the area between the fetlock and heel (particularly on the hind legs), as well as the pasterns, becoming scabby and irritated, this is an indication of dew poisoning. Your veterinarian should be consulted regarding the diagnosis and recommended treatment for this condition, as failure to treat can result in lameness and in either case is painful to the horse.

13. When possible, grain and hay presentation to your horses should be at or near ground level. Their anatomical design equips horses to better eat at ground level since their primary food intake is through grazing. Low feeding tubs and placement of hay at ground level are preferable and will aid in their natural digestion and processing of food. Bear in mind that hay and grain should *not* be placed in sandy nor manure-soiled areas. I personally use goat-feeding bunkers for my grain and try to place hay onto clean grassy areas whenever possible.

14. When approaching your horse with tack, training tools, halters, dewormers, etc., do not make the common mistake of trying to hide the item from your horse. Your effort to initially hide a deworming tube, for instance, will ultimately teach your horse that you cannot be trusted. In addition, prior to the application of tack or the use of grooming tools, it is recommended that you allow the horse to see and smell the item. If the horse is resistant

to the item, continue with the "approach and withdraw" method until the horse is calm and is no longer showing resistance. Do not withdraw the item while the horse is moving away, as this will teach the horse an effective means of avoidance. See the previous chapter regarding the REWARD Technique.

In conclusion, there is no conclusion to the number of common sense tips available for better horse-keeping, and I have attempted to address only a few of the many horse sense methods of horse management for your consideration. Based upon my ongoing life with horses, it is with a humble heart that I submit my thoughts to you; as I continue in my personal horse quest, I look forward to learning and continuing to progress in my own knowledge of both the human *and* the horse. My hope is to be able to share new insights along the way with those God chooses to place in my path.

May all your trails be happy and blessed.

Sample Contracts

Welcome to the world of legal liability! It is with genuine enthusiasm and excitement that you have reached this point. You have your horse—your UBHL—and it is mandatory that you take the necessary precautions to prevent some of the most common legal problems that are certain to present themselves during the course of your life with horses. During your equine quest, you have in all likelihood interacted with a few less than scrupulous business folks; unfortunately, we are well past the era of a hand shake deal and the confidence of a person's word of honor in business. This is sad to consider, but it is reality. We are living in a litigious society wherein it is an absolute requirement for you to place your business agreements into written form. Communication and a clear focus are foremost regarding the terms of your agreements, whether they pertain to equine boarding, training expectations and costs, liability waivers, and bills of sale, just to mention a few of the most frequently encountered equine related contracts.

Although I am including a sample of the contracts used by some of the local barns in my area, I am not an attorney nor do I hold these documents out to be legally binding. You should engage a reputable attorney to review any legal document in order to ensure its validity and to confirm that your interests are protected. The following sample contracts are merely that—samples that are offered so you can adapt them according to your individual needs, recognizing that each state has varying laws pertaining to equine activities.

These particular forms are customized to my state of North Carolina; however, they are not presented as valid, legally binding contracts and should be reviewed by your own personal attorney or qualified legal advisor.

(Name of Business)
Liability Waiver

WARNING! Under North Carolina State law, an equine activity sponsor or equine professional is not liable for an injury to or the death of a participant in equine activities resulting exclusively from the inherent risks of equine activities.

(Chapter 99E of the North Carolina Statutes)

Having read the above North Carolina Statute, and having full understanding and agreement of the inherent risk factors associated with equine activities, I do hereby hold harmless and release from liability (Name of Business or Stable Owner), inclusive of their family members, heirs, and employees any and all claims for damages which may occur as a result of equine related activities on the property located at (address here). This shall include damages for personal injury to myself, my guests and invitees, as well as my horse(s).

Name (Printed): _____

Signature: _____

Date: _____

(Name of Stable)
Equine Boarding Agreement

THIS AGREEMENT, for good and valuable consideration and the receipt of which is hereby acknowledged, dated the _____ day of _____, in the year _____, made by and between (Name of Stable) hereinafter referred to as "STABLE," providing services as an independent contractor, located at (Stable Address Here) and (Equine Owner's Name), residing at (Equine Owner's Address Here), hereinafter referred to as "OWNER." These parties warrant that they have the right to enter into this AGREEMENT.

1. FEES, TERMS, and LOCATION

   In consideration of (Monthly Boarding Fee Here) per horse per month paid by OWNER in advance on the first day of each month, STABLE agrees to board the herein described horse(s) on a month-to-month basis commencing (Date Here). Partial months boarding shall be paid on a pro rata basis based on the numbers of days boarded in a standard thirty-day month.

   Late Fees: Boarding fees paid between the sixth and fifteenth day of the current month due will be subject to a late fee of $15. Fees received after the sixteenth will be subject to a late fee of $25.

2. DESCRIPTION OF HORSE(S)

   Name: _____

   Age: _____

   Color: _____

Registration No/Tattoo/Markings: _____

Sex: _____

Breed: _____

Insurance Carrier, Policy and Phone Number (if applicable): _____

3. FEED AND FACILITIES

STABLE agrees to provide the following, in addition to normal and reasonable care and handling to maintain the health and well-being of the horse(s):

Paddock and/or pasture and run-in shed

Good horse quality forage, feed, water and supplements as per agreement with OWNER

Access and use of round pens, outdoor riding arena, and local STABLE-owned trails

4. VACCINATIONS

Upon arrival of horse(s) to STABLE, proof of current tetanus, sleeping sickness, rabies, and influenza vaccinations is required.

Proof of vaccines are required annually.

A negative current Coggins test is required upon arrival and annually.

5. RISK OF LOSS

During the time that the horse(s) is/are in the custody of STABLE, STABLE shall *not* be liable for any sickness, disease, theft, death, or injury which may be suffered by the horse. This includes, but is not limited to, any personal injury or disability the horse may receive while on STABLE's premises. OWNER fully understands and hereby acknowledges that STABLE does not carry any insurance on any horse not owned by STABLE, including, but not limited to, such insurance for boarding or any other purposes, for which the horse(s) is/are covered under any public liability, accidental injury, theft, or equine mortality insurance, and that all risks relating to boarding of horse(s), or for any other reason, for which the horse(s) is/are in the possession of STABLE, are to be borne by OWNER.

6. HOLD HARMLESS

OWNER agrees to hold STABLE harmless from any claim resulting from damage or injury caused by said horse, OWNER or his guests and invitees, to anyone, including but not limited to legal fees and/or expenses incurred by STABLE in defense of such claims.

7. LIABILITY INSURANCE

OWNER warrants that he/she presently carries in full force and effect, and throughout the period of this AGREEMENT shall continue to carry and maintain in full force and effect, liability insurance protecting OWNER and STABLE from any and all claim(s) arising out of or relating to this AGREEMENT.

8. EMERGENCY CARE

STABLE agrees to attempt to contact OWNER, at the following emergency telephone number (Enter Number Here), should STABLE feel that medical treatment is needed for said horse(s), provided however, that in the event the STABLE is unable to so contact OWNER within a reasonable time, which time shall be judged and determined solely by STABLE, STABLE is then hereby authorized to secure emergency veterinary care and/or blacksmith care, and by any licensed providers of such care who are selected by STABLE, as STABLE determines is required for the health and well-being of said horse(s). The cost of such care secured shall be due and payable by OWNER within fifteen days from the date OWNER receives notice of amount due.

9. STABLE RULES

OWNER hereby acknowledges receipt and understanding of the current STABLE rules, which are incorporated by reference in full, as if fully set forth herein. OWNER agrees he/she and his/her guests and invitees will be bound and abide by these rules, and accepts responsibility for the conduct of his guests and invitees according to these rules. OWNER acknowledges the Rules include but are not limited to:

a. Horses are not to be ridden on lawn and/or driveway areas nor in areas where crops are being produced.

b. OWNER and guests shall be watchful and aware that children may be playing in area and shall take care when working with and/or riding horse, as well as while operating motor vehicles and pulling trailers on property.

c. OWNER shall be respectful of the property of others.

d. OWNER shall be responsible for reconnecting electric fencing if they have disconnected same in order to ride in area.

e. OWNERS and guests are asked to refrain from standing or climbing on gates and fences.

f. NO SMOKING is allowed in stable and riding areas.

g. Trash should be placed in trash receptacles.

h. Normal courtesy and good manners are expected, as well as from STABLE owner, workers and others on property.

i. OWNER and guests are expected to close all gates as they have opened them and to return any tack, equipment or tools used to their respective place.

STABLE may revise these rules from time to time and OWNER agrees any revision shall have the same force and effect as current rules. Failure, as determined in STABLE's sole discretion, or OWNER or OWNER's guests and invitees to abide by STABLE rules may result in STABLE declaring OWNER in default hereunder and result in termination of this AGREEMENT.

10. DEFAULT

Either party may terminate this AGREEMENT for failure of the other party to meet any material terms of this AGREEMENT, including but not limited to item 9 of the stable rules. In the case of failure by either party to fulfill AGREEMENT terms, a verbal communication in regard to the matter should be offered in an effort to cure the default. In the event a verbal communication is not feasible or possible, a written letter explaining the complaint should be submitted, allowing a reasonable amount of time to effect cure prior to termination of AGREEMENT. If the appropriate cure is not accomplished, the other party shall have the right to recover legal fees and expenses, if any, incurred as a result of said default. Any payment due STABLE under this AGREEMENT shall be due and payable by the tenth day of the month and immediately in the event of termination. Failure to make any payment by said due date shall place OWNER in default hereunder. Acceptance by STABLE of any late payment shall not constitute a waiver of subsequent due dates or determinations of default. Any prepayment of boarding fees will be prorated and refunded to OWNER.

11. ASSIGNMENT

This AGREEMENT may not be assigned by OWNER without the express written consent of STABLE.

12. NOTICE OF TERMINATION

OWNER agrees that thirty (30) days notice shall be given to STABLE as to the termination of this AGREEMENT.

13. RIGHT OF LIEN

OWNER is put on notice that STABLE has and may assert and exercise a right of lien, as provided for by the laws of the state of North Carolina for any amount due for the board and keep of horse(s), and also for any storage or other charges due hereunder, and further agrees STABLE shall have the right, without process of law, to attach a lien to your horse(s) after two (2) months of non-payment or partial payment and STABLE can then sell horse(s) to recover its loss.

14. SPECIAL INSTRUCTIONS TO STABLE

THIS AGREEMENT IS SUBJECT TO THE LAWS OF THE state of North Carolina. Executed at (STABLE Name Here) on the date first set forth above.

By: (Authorized Representative/Owner of STABLE) Signature and Date:

_____

OWNER Signature and Date:

_____

Owner's Address:

_____

Day Phone:

_____

Evening Phone:

_____

Equine Lease Agreement

THIS AGREEMENT entered into as of (Current Date Here) between (Horse Owner Name Here), hereinafter referred to as OWNER, residing at (Owner Address Here) and (Lessee Name Here), hereinafter referred to as LESSEE, residing at (Lessee Address Here).

WITNESSETH: OWNER does hereby lease to LESSEE and LESSEE does hereby lease from the OWNER the (Enter Description of Horse/Gender) known as (Enter Horse's Legal and/or Common Name and Registration No. if Applicable). The lease shall be for a period of time beginning (Enter Beginning Date) continuing on a month to month basis until termination of AGREEMENT by either party. Termination of AGREEMENT shall require written notice of not less than thirty (30) days prior to termination date.

In exchange for the exclusive use of the above-named horse during the period of this lease, the LESSEE does hereby agree to pay to OWNER the amount of (Enter Dollar Amount) per month. In addition, LESSEE as well as guests and invitees of LESSEE will be entitled to participate in riding, grooming, bathing, feeding, and any other equine-related activities which they deem appropriate on the premises of OWNER at (Stable Location Here). LESSEE will be expected to clean the horse's stall/shed no less than twice weekly, and riders are expected to follow normal stable rules as well as OWNER's natural horsemanship practices, including the proper grooming and care necessary both before and following riding activities.

OWNER shall be responsible for all continuing care and upkeep expenses for said horse and horse shall continue to reside on the property of OWNER. This shall include, but is not limited to, all forage, feed, worming, veterinary expenses, and hoof trimming as well as any other expenses which are consistent with the practices of good animal husbandry.

OWNER shall require and provide no less than one riding lesson per week for each rider, at the rate of (Enter Dollar Amount Here) per lesson.

OWNER shall provide at no additional charge to LESSEE a proper saddle, bridle, and necessary tack to be used for riding, as well as grooming and barn tools.

For no additional fee and with prior notice, LESSEE is entitled to enter onto property and is allowed full use of all horse-related facilities as described herein at any time during the period of this lease. This is inclusive, but is not limited to the barn facilities for the purpose of break time as necessary.

All children under the age of fourteen must be supervised at all times by an adult unless otherwise agreed between OWNER and LESSEE. All riders must wear approved riding helmets and proper shoes for safety. All posted barn rules and rules of common courtesy and respect are to be followed by LESSEE, guests and invitees of LESSEE, as well as by OWNER.

A LIABILITY WAIVER is herein incorporated and attached as Exhibit A. In addition, OWNER shall not hold LESSEE liable for any serious injury or death of the horse arising from events not resulting from negligence on the part of the LESSEE or the LESSEE's agents.

LESSEE shall hold the OWNER harmless for any injury or death to persons or damages to any property caused by the leased horse.

LESSEE warrants that he/she has inspected said horse and agrees to accept said horse in present condition. LESSEE will not be entitled to transport the horse off the OWNER's property without prior written authorization by OWNER.

The title and ownership of the leased horse shall be and remain in the name of the OWNER. LESSEE shall not sell, mortgage, or encumber this leased horse in any manner whatsoever. LESSEE shall not assign this lease nor sublease the horse covered hereby.

No modification of this lease shall be binding unless in writing and executed by the parties herein.

The undersigned OWNER and LESSEE accept the terms and conditions of this lease and acknowledge a copy thereof.

OWNER:

_____

(Signature and Date):

LESSEE:

_____

(Signature and Date):

Epilogue

My goal in writing this book, as I have expressed earlier, is an attempt to address and inform other horse enthusiasts in regard to a few of the more common horse-related and problematic issues, thereby assisting my readers in making better equine choices and decisions. I have certainly learned from my own mistakes, and hope others will be able to avoid these foreseeable pitfalls.

My life with horses has certainly impacted my life in general, both personally and as it relates to business. During these past few years, I have experienced great loss through the death of my mother in 1999 and the long-term disability of my dad and ultimately his death in 2006. In addition, my marriage as well as my successful, family-owned marketing business—both twenty plus years in the running—came to an unexpected demise.

As a result, I found myself with the challenge of starting over in my personal life as well as in my career; my love of horses together with my childhood life on the farm presented an obvious God-given opportunity for me. I have been able to apply my business education and experience-enlightened equine skills and knowledge toward the development of our little farm to include horse training and breeding, natural horsemanship instruction, horse boarding, and equine-related consultation services. Although the trail toward success is patchy and somewhat difficult, my personal relationship with Jesus Christ as my Savior has enabled me to maintain my focus, and in spite of the downward economic trend in play at this time in our country, I can still envision success; there is always hope in Christ and a brilliant light toward which I direct both my business and personal path.

In addition, my family has always been supportive of my business and equine endeavors, although I recognize that the significant time and economic challenge of operating a horse farm has certainly impacted their lives as well. My two adult children and their spouses, my five grandchildren, and my new husband as well have all indulged me with the offer of their time and services when able, as well as in the allowance of the family time sacrificed which I have had to devote toward the equine business and farm upkeep. I thank them from the bottom of my heart for their love and support. God has truly blessed me with a wonderful family.

I would be remiss if I failed to mention how many times my equine family has come to my aid on those days when life seemed to be most dreary. Their ability to sense our personal energy includes their perception of sadness as well. After my dad's funeral, I recall sitting on an overturned bucket in the horse pasture while waiting for water tubs to fill, experiencing a sense of sadness I had not previously known to exist. Twinkle (the world's best pony ever), walked over to my side and laid her head on my shoulder. Hugging her to me, I looked up to see huge "pony tears" rolling down her cheeks. This was one of many instances wherein I recognized that horses and humans *are* able to communicate and in some cases provide comfort and support within a network of trust.

God, Family, Friends, Horses
I am truly blessed.

Acknowledgments

Most of the enclosed photographs were taken on our farm here at Gentle Spirit Stables in Bailey, North Carolina, by my daughter, Frieda Craft Eakins and my son, M. Ryan Craft, both of whom are gifted with the "eye" of a photographer. They have both grown into fine adults who reflect the love of Christ and who are certainly the light of my life. I love them and appreciate them more than they will ever know.

Ephesians 1:15–23